Powerboat Racing on the Chesapeake

By William W. Mowbray

TIDEWATER PUBLISHERS

Centreville, Maryland

Front cover: John Fitzgerald in the *Leprechaun* (J-90) leads Sarge Johnson of Cambridge in his *Sarge's Barge* coming out of the second turn during the 1982 Cambridge Classic Regatta. Photograph by Tom Kelly.

Back cover: Shown taking a turn in the Jersey Speed Skiff *Selfish Pleasure* is driver Bill Salveson of Clermont, New Jersey, with riding mechanic Tom Herchenrider of King of Prussia, Pennsylvania. Photograph by Tom Kelly.

Library of Congress Cataloging-in-Publication Data

Mowbray, William.
Powerboat racing on the Chesapeake / by William W. Mowbray. —1st ed.
p. cm.
Includes index.
ISBN 0-87033-473-5 (PB)
1. Motorboat racing—Chesapeake Bay Region (Md. and Va.)
2. Chesapeake Bay Region (Md. and Va.)—Guidebooks. I. Title.
GV835.9.M67 1995
796.1'25'0916347—dc20 95-44185
CIP

Manufactured in the United States of America
First edition

Powerboat Racing on the Chesapeake

To Mary Isabelle Wilkinson Mowbray

Contents

Preface

The first twelve years of my life were spent living in a house one block from the Choptank River in Cambridge, Maryland. I can remember my mother always telling me as I went outside to play, "Remember, you are not to leave the yard." Well, the yard in my mind encompassed all the territory from the front of our Maryland Avenue house to the river shore, and the backyard stretched about one-half mile to the old Phillips Packing Company buildings on old Route 50.

Most of the neighborhood kids back then spent summer days playing sandlot baseball, cowboys and Indians, and in numerous activities on and around the Choptank River. We had fun swimming, boating, crabbing, fishing, and—to the horror of our parents—climbing onto the Emerson C. Harrington Bridge and diving from the pilings or the span into our beloved Choptank. It has often been said that many of us could swim before we could walk.

The Choptank was a vital social and recreational aspect of our lives in the 1940s and 1950s. I have no recollection of any swimming pools in Dorchester County at the time, but the Red Cross sponsored swimming lessons at various beaches in the area.

Sometime during the summer of 1945 when I was five years old, I remember hearing strange, loud sounds coming from somewhere on the river. I went to my second-story bedroom, where I had a beautiful and strategic vantage point to see miles of the Choptank, and noticed what appeared to be tidal waves of water near the bridge. I asked my mother what these strange sights and sounds were, and she explained that the annual boat races were being held. The next day we walked out on the bridge, and to my absolute delight I got a close-up view of dozens of thunderous, speeding hydroplanes racing around a course in

A pair of 5-liter hydroplanes spurt "roostertails" as they roar off a turn on Hambrooks Bay in Cambridge.

front of the Cambridge Yacht Club. These speeding boats appeared to be gushing tons of water into the air behind them, which I later learned were called roostertails. My introduction to the sport of powerboat racing had begun. From that point until today—about fifty years—I think I have missed only three or four of the powerboat racing weekends in Cambridge.

There is extensive documented history of the Chesapeake Bay and its reputation as a boating heaven. Books, magazines, and journals provide a wealth of information regarding the Bay and the boating industry, but one aspect of the Bay boating tradition that is not well documented is the sport of powerboat racing. I visited a large bookstore a few years ago and found a huge selection of books on Chesapeake Bay boating: books on cruising, shiphandling, marine electronics, seamanship, navigation, yachting, sailing, yacht design, model boats, chartering, boatbuilding, and marinas. Typical topics in these books included design, planning, buying, refurbishing, and repairing. What I did not find, however, was a single book, or even a single chapter in a book, relating to the sport of powerboat racing. Since I have a deep devotion to the sport of powerboat racing and a love of the Chesapeake Bay, I decided that it was time for someone to gather pertinent data on the sport and record its history as well as its impact on the recreational boating industry in the Bay area.

For their help in this endeavor, I want to thank Ed Nabb, Harold Ruark, George Cusick, Skeeter Johnson, Ed Thompson, and Wheeler Baker. And a very special thanks to those racers, so familiar to Chesapeake Bay racing fans, who loved the sport far more than I and made the supreme sacrifice in doing what they enjoyed doing so much: Eddie Cannon, Homer Bland, Hank Lauterbach, Dean Chenoweth, Lew Coehler, Frank Connally, Paul Flohn, Bill Heath, Mac Jordan, Frank Kossow, Tillman Mohr, Bill Muncey, Ron Musson, Jack McMahon, Bob Presley, Dave Sooy, and Dickie Webb.

The late Jay Wheatley of Cambridge prepares to work on the 283-cubic-inch Chevrolet engine of his Jersey Speed Skiff Mud Flat Missile II *prior to Chesapeake Bay Regatta at Kent Island.*

Powerboat Racing on the Chesapeake

Doug Masengale of Crofton, Maryland, in his 2.5-liter modified hydroplane Little Red Rocket. *Photograph by Tom Kelly*

1

Powerboat Racing: The Early Pioneers

Before getting to the subject of racing, some general information on the development of the internal combustion engine as used in power boating may be helpful. Several piston and pistonless steam engines were developed as early as the late 1600s, but James Watt set the basic pattern of all subsequent reciprocating steam engines in about 1770. The first internal combustion engine was designed by German engineer Nikolaus Otto in 1867. Eighteen years later, Karl-Friedrich Benz built the first successful gas-driven vehicle. It was only a matter of time before the technology that brought us the automobile was applied to boats.

Most internal combustion engines as we know them involve the four-stroke cycle: (1) intake, which is a stroke down to draw a gasoline-air mixture into the cylinder; (2) compression, which is a stroke up to squeeze or compress the fuel mixture and during which time an electric spark ignites the fuel; (3) power, which is a stroke down to deliver power from the burned and expanded gases to the crankshaft; and (4) exhaust, which is a stroke up to push out the burned gases.

Engines are of two main types: inboard and outboard. Inboard engines are usually gasoline, liquid or air-cooled, or diesel models. They are located amidships and connected to the propeller by a slanting shaft that passes through the bottom of the boat. Outboard engines operate on the same principle as other gasoline engines, but incorporate the complete propulsion train, from motor to propeller, in a portable unit. The outboard engine is usually fastened to the boat's stern or transom with a hinged mounting so that the propeller can be raised when not in use.

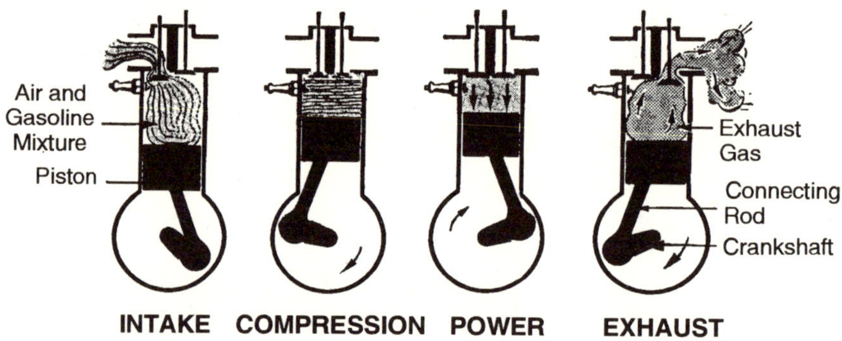

Four-stroke cycle gasoline engine.

The American Power Boat Association

In this book, I will refer frequently to subjects related to "official" powerboat racing, by which I mean racing that has been sanctioned by the American Power Boat Association (APBA). I will also be using the names of specific classes of racing, which will be familiar to most Chesapeake Bay area powerboat racing fans, but probably an enigma to those with little exposure to the sport.

Therefore, here is a quick primer on some of the classes of powerboats. Although there are several categories of racing under the auspices of the APBA, I will concentrate primarily on the limited inboard division, which has proven to be the most popular over the years in the Chesapeake region.

Classes are generally referred to by the maximum engine displacement, or volume of water being displaced, allowed in a particular class. A 1–liter stock hydroplane, for example, is allowed a maximum engine displacement of 1,200 cubic centimeters, whereas a 6-liter hydroplane is allowed 368 cubic inches. In terms of both engine and hull size, the classes I will be discussing most are (in order of size): 1-liter hydroplane, 2.5-liter stock hydroplane, 2.5-liter modified hydroplane, 5-liter stock hydroplane, 6-liter hydroplane, and 7-liter, or Grand National, hydroplane. In classes where the term "stock" is used, it means that a stock automotive engine as furnished by the motor manufacturer is required whereas if a class is described as "modified," it means that stock parts may be changed at the discretion of the engine builder.

Another class will also be mentioned frequently: runabouts, which are sometimes referred to as "flatbottoms." These boats are unlike hydroplanes in that they do not have sponsons, but are rather like a flat-bottom pleasure boat. A complete chart of the inboard class specifications is found on page 6.

Origins of the APBA and UIM

Powerboat racing originated officially at the turn of the century with the establishment of the American Power Boat Association. No doubt, there were many races long before APBA came into existence, but since no formal organization had been founded to oversee them, there were no rules and regulations and little documentation. With the founding of APBA, however, records and rules for the sport are now well documented.

APBA Powerboat Limited Inboard Classes				
Hydroplanes				
Class	*Letter*	*Length in Feet*	*Maximum Engine Displacement*	*Weight Limit*
1.5-Liter	Z	14	1200cc-1587cc	650
2.5-Liter Stock	S	13.5	2300cc	850 (w/driver)
2.5-Liter Modified	A	16	155.5 c.i.	1,000
4-Liter Modified	N	16	246 c.i.	1,100
5-Liter	E	16	305 c.i.	1,200
6-Liter	F	19	368 c.i.	1,400
7-Liter (Grand National)	GNH	20	454 c.i.	1,800
Grand Prix	GP	20-21	500 c.i.	2,200-2,400
Runabouts				
Cracker Box	P	13.5-15.5	275 c.i.	1,250
K Racing Runabout	K	17	Unlimited	None
Pro Stock	PS	16-20	500 c.i.	None
Super Stock	SS	16	428 c.i.	None
Jersey Speed Skiff	JS	16	305 c.i.	1,600
Competition Jet	CJ	16	500 c.i.	None

Since powerboat owners, whether in a workboat, fishing craft, or pleasure boat, have always taken pride in how fast their boats would run, there has always been racing among them. Eventually there were enough people interested only in the speed of the boat that special racing boats were developed. These crafts were of no value for fishing or waterskiing. You certainly couldn't make a living dredging for oysters in them. And they were hardly cost-

Gee McClain of Cambridge guides his super stock runabout April *down the backstretch. Photograph by Tom Kelly*

efficient for taking long cruises. They were built for speed, and it became an obsession among their owners to lay claim to having the fastest boat. Prior to 1903, there was little consideration given to the size of the boat or the size or type of its engine. There were no rules, and therefore, parity was nonexistent.

According to one account of the events that led to organized powerboat racing, about the turn of the century a group of powerboaters around New York's Long Island Sound wanted to race their boats officially. The *1988 APBA Reference Book* reads: "By 1902 there were enough of these crafts around to stimulate an interest among their owners as to which boat could travel fastest over a given distance with a given handicap. In short, people wanted to race their boats."

But there were many varieties of inboard and outboard engines, a wide range of hull designs, and an even larger number of opinions as to how to come up with an equalizing method for fair racing. Obviously rules would have to be introduced to "handicap all boats equally." Members of the Columbia Yacht Club called a series of meetings, and, finally, on April 22, 1903, the American Power Boat Association was formed. Rules were set, officers elected, and a constitution adopted. In 1924, with the emergence of outboard motors, a new outboard division was added. Today APBA conducts organized racing for all types of powerboats, from the unlimited class to the family outboard runabout. Approximately four hundred regattas are sanctioned each year in the United States, with more than four thousand registered race boats.

International powerboat racing is conducted under the jurisdiction of the Union of International Motorboating (UIM). The UIM, founded in 1922, is headquartered in Monaco. According to the *APBA Reference Book*: "In each country one powerboat racing organization is designated by UIM as the national authority. In the United States, the American Power Boat Association is recognized by UIM as the national authority and governing body for organized racing."

The first competition for powerboats under APBA rules was the Gold Challenge Cup, conducted in June 1904 at the Columbia Yacht Club on the Hudson River. C.C. Riotte piloted the 59-foot *Standard* at an average speed of 23.61 miles per hour for 32 one-mile heats to defeat two other competitors. Fifteen years later, famed driver Gar Wood of the Detroit Yacht Club drove his *Miss America* to a Gold Cup victory averaging 71.3 miles per hour. Today, with their turbine engines, the unlimited hydroplanes travel at approximately 200 miles per hour.

The first National Motor Boat Show was held in New York at Madison Square Garden in 1905. That year, there were fewer than 20,000 pleasure boats—sail and motor combined—in the United

Chestertown had one of the most popular races in the Chesapeake Bay region for a number of years. Shown are two hydroplanes going into turn one.

States. Most of those were owned by wealthy Americans. By 1990, a survey showed more than 8,850,000 recreational boats registered, of which 6,200,000 were motorboats. According to that survey, an estimated fifty million Americans engaged in some form of boating each year.

Powerboat Racing Categories

APBA has several categories of racing, which include the following:

1. Inboard—This division includes both hydroplanes and runabouts, or flatbottoms. Engine sizes range from 1-liter stock automotive to 500 cubic inches. Speeds up to 170 miles per hour are attained.

2. Unlimited—These monsters are called the "thunderboats" and, as the category name states, have unlimited horsepower. Most of the unlimiteds today use helicopter turbine engines, so

the term “thunderboat” is hardly an accurate description any longer since the turbines make a whining noise. However, a few Rolls-Royce Merlins, Griffons, and Allisons are still around to produce the “thunderous” noise of a piston engine with no muffler. Any fuel is permitted in this class; the boats generate 3,000 horsepower and attain speeds over 200 miles per hour.

3. Outboard—The most popular avenue to enter powerboat racing is in this division, which is most economical in the stock outboard category. The stock outboard category uses all off-the-shelf equipment, which makes it less expensive. Other outboard categories include professional racing outboard (offers competitors the greatest latitude in altering their equipment and burning special fuels containing alcohol), outboard performance craft (features tunnel boats which are a combination of a hydroplane and a flatbottom), and modified outboard (similar to stock, but have modified engines).

4. Offshore—As the name implies, these boats perform offshore, often in the ocean. The boats usually are catamarans or deep V-style hulls and they carry a driver, throttleman, and navigator.

Other classes include inboard endurance and drag. Inboard endurance is a distance event category in which the driver and the equipment are tested for a marathon race. The drag boat category is exactly what its name implies: drag racers race the clock over a straight, quarter-mile course.

Records, Championships, and Honors

Until 1994 APBA recognized both a “national champion” and a “national high point champion,” but this arrangement had always had its critics—both competitors and fans. Pre-1994 national champions were crowned based on the performance of a boat at one designated “national championship” regatta. The national high point champion was crowned based on the total number of points that boat accumulated over the course of an entire season of racing. There was always controversy as to which of the two awards held more meaning; in addition, many felt the arrangement was confusing for boat-racing fans. APBA now awards the national championship to the boat with the highest total of points over the season (November 1 to October 31) in its class. There is no longer a national high point champion.

Another title boat racers pursue is the North American championship. This championship, which is cosponsored by APBA, CBF (Canadian Boating Federation), and FMM (Federation Mexicana de Montonautica), is decided at a regatta held each year in one of the three North American countries.

There are two approved speed record categories for powerboat racing: a world record and a national or APBA record. Records must be set on APBA-approved racecourses of a mile or a mile-and-a-quarter distance. These are referred to as five-mile competition records (an official APBA race consists of five miles). On a one-mile approved course five laps are required and on a mile-and-a-quarter-approved course four laps must be run. Record times are determined to the thousandth of a second and miles per hour are calculated to three decimal places in the formula. The one-mile formula is as follows:

Miles per hour = 3,600 ÷ time

There is also a kilo or straightaway record. This is a noncompetition record (the boat does not run against other boats, but against the clock only) where a boat must make two consecutive one-mile straightaway runs. The formula is as follows:

Miles per hour = 2,236.936 ÷ time

Among other accolades awarded to participants in powerboat racing are nomination to either the APBA Honor Squadron or the APBA Hall of Champions. The APBA Honor Squadron was founded in 1953 as a feature of APBA's fiftieth anniversary. The association wished to honor outstanding individuals for distin-

American Power Boat Association • Records as of October 31, 1994

Class	*Type of Record*	*Speed (MPH)*	*Date & Location*	*Boat Name & Owner*	*Driver*	*Hull and Engine*
7-Liter	Kilo	155.718	10-19-91/Lincoln City, OR	*Enterprise*/Three Roses, Inc.	Brad Mosier	Hanson/Chevrolet
7-Liter	5Mi/3 Lap	117.058	9-5-87/Essex, MD	*Miss Stroh's Beer*/PrimeMover Ent.	Wheeler Baker	Staudacher/Ford
7-Liter	5Mi/4 Lap	112.016	4-17-88/St. Petersburg, FL	*Miss Stroh's Light*/PrimeMover Ent.	Tom Baker	Staudacher/Ford
7-Liter	5Mi/5 Lap	97.161	9-22-91/Yelm, WA	*Enterprise*/Three Roses, Inc.	Brad Mosier	Hanson/Chevrolet
6-Liter	Kilo	152.130	10-30-71/Parker, AZ	*Going Thing*/John Wolf	Mickey Remund	R. Jones/Ford
6-Liter	5Mi/5 Lap	91.190	7-29-90/Sylvan Lake, MI	*Miss Toledo*/Carl Haas	Randy Haas	R. Jones/Chevrolet
2.5-Liter Mod	Kilo	132.769	9-30-89/Lincoln City, OR	*In Cahoots*/John Devos	John Devos	Staudacher/BMW
2.5-Liter Mod	5Mi/5 Lap	88.6	10-21-90/Portsmouth, VA	*Miss Aquamet*/Marine Racing	Wheeler Baker	Staudacher/Ford
5-Liter	Kilo	124.123	4-9-83/Moore Haven, FL	*Last Blast II*/Everett Gillam	William Coker	Karelsen/Plymouth
5-Liter	5Mi/5 Lap	82.320	7-31-88/Sylvan Lake, MI	*Miss Zeroll*/Thomas Funka	Mark Tate	R. Jones/Chevrolet
2.5-Liter Stock	Kilo	105.333	11-27-82/Parker, AZ	*Rich Coutts Special*/Wm. Mattocks	Dennis Mattocks	Jones/Ford Pinto
2.5-Liter Stock	5 Mi/5 Lap	77.888	9-20-92/St. Petersburg, FL	*Lobster Boat*/Bobby Weaver	Bobby Weaver	Tone/Ford
1-Liter Stock	Kilo	95.920	3-19-89/Moore Haven, FL	*Good to Go*/Paul Mezyk	Paul Mezyk	Gillam/Toyota
1-Liter Stock	5 Mi/5 Lap	66.780	10-5-91/Portsmouth, VA	*Constant Pressure*/Ron Smith	Steve David	Blide/Toyota
1-Liter Mod	Kilo	102.263	4-4-82/Moore Haven, FL	*Century 21 Special*/Steve David	Steve David	Kelson/Sunbeam
1-Liter Mod	5 Mi/5 Lap	71.727	5-4-91/Kent, WA	*Supply & Demand*/Charley Wiggins	Charley Wiggins	Jones/Toyota
JSS	Kilo	83.019	3-18-89/Moore Haven, FL	*Flat Flyin*/Robert Birdsall	Robert Birdsall	Baron/Chevrolet
JSS	5 Mi/5 Lap	67.484	9-20-92/St. Petersburg, FL	*Flat Flyin*/Robert Birdsall	Robert Birdsall	Baron/Chevrolet
SuperStock	Kilo	115.664	5-30-80/Parker, AZ	*Crown It*/J.W. Cooper	Gordon Jennings	Barron/Chevrolet
SuperStock	5 Mi/5 Lap	89.548	9-28-91/Oroville, CA	*Stars & Stripes*/Samma Thompson	Gordon Jennings	Biesmeyer/Pfaff
Pro Stock	Kilo	127.754	11-24-89/Parker, AZ	*Steeler*/Duff Daily	Duff Daily	D'Cucci/Chrysler
Pro Stock	5 Mi/3 Lap	101.129	9-5-87/Essex, MD	*Sweet Caroline*/John Kiely, Jr.	Gee McClain	Revenge/Chevrolet
Pro Stock	5 Mi/5 Lap	83.515	5-14-88/West Milford, NJ	*Mad Dog*/James Nader	James Nader	Revenge/Chevrolet

Source: *APBA 1995 Reference Book*

guished contributions to the sport of powerboat racing. Selection for the Honor Squadron is considered the highest of APBA's awards. Participants from all areas of the sport of powerboat racing are considered for membership: drivers, owners, designers, builders, and engineers, as well as organizers and officials. A special APBA committee, including several prominent boating journalists, is in charge of guidelines for selecting the three individuals inducted annually.

The APBA Hall of Champions was established in 1974 by APBA to distinguish its most outstanding drivers from each season. This award program replaced what was known for many years as The Gulf Marine Racing Hall of Fame. The two most important factors considered for induction into the Hall of Champions are total points accumulated during the course of the season and whether or not a speed record was attained.

The State of Maryland Athletic Hall of Fame was founded by the University of Maryland M Club in 1955. The objective of this award is to honor Maryland athletes who have distinguished themselves in sports competition. Four boat racers are currently in the Maryland Hall of Fame: Don Christy, Alton Pierson, Skeeter Johnson, and George Cusick.

On the Money Side of the Sport

Because I really appreciated the writer's viewpoint, I have saved for years a portion of an article in which the now-unknown author states: "Nobody ever said that boat racing was supposed to be an inexpensive sport. From a purely financial standpoint, weighing all the costs against what might be recovered in the way of prize money, you better love the sport because it's a certainty that your banker and bookkeeper won't. Of course, just about anything you do for recreation has its price tag—big or small. When you look at the overall picture, however, boat racing has some definite positive aspects. The most attractive feature is the wide range of involvement levels. You can either spend a lot or a little; it depends on how serious you want to be and how fast you want to go."

On the least costly end of the spectrum are the stock outboard classes in which an investment of as little as $1,000 will get you on the water and into organized competition (in a small hull with a low horsepower outboard). The stock outboard class of racing is also extremely popular among competitors in the Chesapeake Bay area. The Denton, Maryland, race still draws a large field of drivers. Scott Hoffman of Ocean City, Maryland; Richard Hoenen of Lewes, Delaware; and the Augustine family are among the most successful stock outboard racers in the region racing in this class. Don Christy of Baltimore, a former champion outboard racer, was inducted into the State of Maryland Athletic Hall of Fame in 1980, the first powerboat racer to be so honored.

At the other extreme, you have your mega-motor and mega-buck offshore boats, and the awesome, unlimited hydroplanes for which a tidy million in greenbacks is just the ante. The unlimited division is the corporate-sponsored end of powerboat racing and may be compared to the Winston Cup division of NASCAR automobile racing.

In between are all the other classes of boats, ranging from outboards, to drag boats, to inboard circle racers.

Knowledge Translates into Performance

There has always been a economic or profit incentive for boatbuilders to produce different types of hulls and hull materials. Generally, what proves to be successful and popular for racers, crosses over to recreational boating. Changes in boat design to improve performance have endless possibilities and development continues to this day.

Prior to World War II racing for substantial-sized boats was popular, and all sorts and shapes of craft were tried. This experimentation provided practical knowledge of how specific hull forms reacted to being driven hard at sea, and the results were incorporated into the sport. The offshore category of powerboat racing, for example, has two basic types of hull design for racing in rough waters: the deep V-style hull and the catamaran style. The V-style is designed to "cut through the water," whereas the catamaran (two hulls constructed side by side) travels over the water similar to a hydroplane. These types of boats are no strangers to the Chesapeake Bay where many Cigarette and Scarub "muscle boats" can be seen on most any weekend. While these particular boats are built for performance and speed, the same basic designs with modifications can also provide the general public with a high-performance pleasure boat that is also comfortable even in fairly rough water. Donald J. Aronow of Coral Cables, Florida, built many offshore racing boats bearing the names of Donzi, Formula, Magnum, and Cigarette (all were deep-V constructed). He later named his company The Cigarette Boat Co. The Cigarette boats were about 40 feet long, but very skinny (approximately 8 feet). The Scarub Boat Co. built boats that were very similar to the Cigarette design.

Choosing the material for the construction design of a racing boat requires consideration of the numerous alternatives: wood, aluminum alloy, Kevlar, fiberglass. The strength of the material is perhaps the most important aspect, but cost and availability must also be considered. Over the long term, wood has been the most common material in structural work and planking for boats. The weight of the wood is extremely important due to the critical power/weight ratio. Oak, elm, and teak are not suitable because those types of wood are too heavy. Some wood, such as birch, for example, is not practical because it is prone to rot.

Planking used by early boatbuilders was usually mahogany and Sitka spruce. Plywood came along about 1942 and, due to the fact it was light in weight and plentiful, it became the most popular choice among race boat builders. The plywood planking had to be glued together, however, and also treated against rot.

Over a period of time builders learned that the glue utilized in the construction was as important as the plywood itself.

Aluminum alloy was tried in 1946, and, although it was strong and light, it was also very expensive and had to be welded or riveted together so it never found many proponents in the racing community. Fiberglass and the closely related resinglass were used by race boat builders in the 1950s; these materials performed well when used properly, but their use can be tricky business. Controlled conditions such as temperature and humidity have to be closely observed when working with a glass product. The advantages of these products are low maintenance and strength as compared with wood. Dick Bertrum is credited by some with having the first fiberglass race boat built in 1954, but

Plywood hydroplanes were popular in the late forties and fifties. These are 136-inch hydros. Photograph by Bobby Layton

my research credits Gordon Hoover with that honor in 1959. Hoover raced his 27-foot fiberglass *Chrystaliner* in the Miami to Nassau race that year, finishing second to Bertrum in the *Moppy*. Bertrum's first glass boat, *Glass Moppy*, was built in 1961 and driven by Sam Griffith.

A new material, similar to a clear plastic, was developed by the DuPont Company in 1971; Kevlar is stronger than glass and about half the weight. It is a fiber five times stronger than steel, which was invented by a chemist named Stephanie L. Kwolek. Kevlar is used primarily as a laminating reinforcement. A hull reinforced with Kevlar will be 10 to 30 percent lighter than one with fiberglass alone. Kevlar is still used frequently in the construction of most types of boats, for both racing and pleasure.

Consideration of the type of design a race boat will take depends not only on the construction material, but also upon the type of water on which the boat will race (lakes, rivers, oceans, salt water, or fresh water) and the kind of use (racing short distances, endurance racing, straightaway racing, oval racing) to which the boat will be put. For example, V-hulls and catamarans can handle most conditions, but hydroplanes are restricted by their shape to racing at high speed only on relatively smooth water.

Fundamental physical properties also affect the action of a boat on the water and the design of a racing boat. Water is a viscous fluid, so there are basically two kinds of resistance to the forward motion of a boat: frictional and wave-making. The boat expends its horsepower in overcoming these forces.

Frictional resistance simply means that it will take some energy to push a boat through water due to the friction on the boat's wetted surface. All underwater objects—the bottom, the skid fin, the rudder, and the propeller—must be taken into account when determining frictional resistance since they are all a part of the wetted surface. Wave-making resistance is not as simple to describe; it is a technical calculation of the speed of the boat, the length of the wave created as a result of the boat pushing the water aside, and the speed/length ratio. But some comparisons are easy to make; for example, the wave-making resistance of a speeding hydroplane is far less than that of a V-bottom boat.

Both types of resistance may best be illustrated by watching a hydroplane attempt to get on plane (moving along on top of the water) from a dead stop. Initially, the frictional resistance makes it difficult for the boat to get "up" as it pushes water aside. You can hear the engine revolutions accelerate as the boat tries to

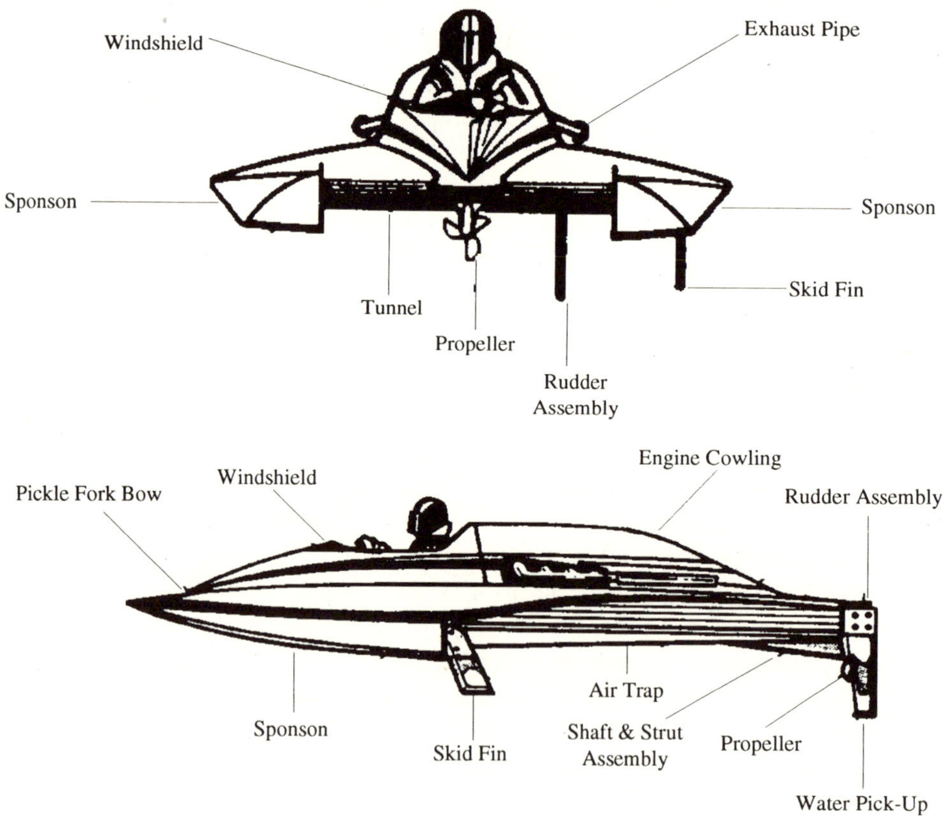

Nomenclature of a hydroplane

Tom Baker in his Bo's Ghost *at a race in Valleyfield, Quebec, Canada, in 1976 demonstrates the "prop-rider" effect of a hydroplane. Photograph by Tom Kelly*

push the water aside. Once the boat is on plane, the wave-making resistance can be observed. At the early low speed the wash is heavy, but it will gradually subside as the boat rises out of the water.

A boat will displace only its own weight in water. In other words, the weight of a boat, with all its fittings, engine, fuel, and driver, will equal its displacement. It is not uncommon to hear a boat racer complain about his own weight since he has added to the displacement, which will slow the speed of the boat. Displacement is also one of the reasons why APBA has minimum weight restrictions in each category of racing. The lighter the boat, the more dangerous it becomes at high speed.

How the boat rides in or across the water is a major factor in powerboat racing. The so-called "prop-rider" effect, in which only the propeller is to be immersed, gradually evolved as the fastest method for a hull to skim across water. Credited primarily to Adolph Apel in the 1940s, the three-point suspension hydroplane is often regarded as the most innovative feature in the development of powerboat racing. As the name hydroplane implies, the object is meant to "fly across the water" as opposed to driving through it. Apel is credited with designing a stepped bottom, which raises the hull wholly, or partly, out of the water. The sponsons serve to keep the boat stable while only the propeller, or prop, is actually in the water. The term "three-point-suspension" refers to the two sponsons and the stern of a race boat which make contact with the water. The three points free up air under the hull to allow the boat to "fly" across the water. Later the "prop-rider" effect took hold as the stern was lifted out of the water with only the sponsons and prop coming in contact with the water.

Hydroplane racing is generally what most people think of when one mentions powerboat racing, and nowhere in America is hydroplane racing so deeply rooted in tradition than in the Chesapeake Bay region.

Bobby Brown of Parsonsburg, Maryland, in the 5-liter hydroplane Cloud Nine *battles Greg Williams of Joppa, Maryland, in Ron Thompson's* Hot to Trot.
Photograph by Tom Kelly

2

Chesapeake Bay Races Among the Best

Although APBA sanctions official regattas throughout the United States, in this book we will be concentrating on the Chesapeake Bay area of Region Four of APBA, which includes Maryland, Virginia, the District of Columbia, West Virginia, and North Carolina.

Powerboat regattas, or races, in the Chesapeake Bay region can be traced back at least as far as 1906, when a regatta on the Miles River in St. Michaels was documented. Apparently, those races were sponsored by the Chesapeake Bay Yacht Club of Easton and included several types of power and sailing craft. An account of one such regatta in August of 1906 referred to racing canoes measuring 29 and 36 feet and 26 and 36 feet to load waterline, and also to motor races on an eight-mile course. The winner of the latter was *Fairbanks of Baltimore*, driven by Captain Thomas Lasell, with a time of 39 minutes.

Years ago there were as many as ten races a year in the Chesapeake Bay area. In those early days of racing, and up until the late 1950s, it was customary, and to some a ritual, for Chesapeake Bay yacht clubs to schedule cruises each weekend to an area regatta. During each of the regional regattas, all of the Bay clubs would form huge "spectator fleets" and plan a complete weekend of festivities around the racing activities. Local merchants would have special "Racing Dollar Days" in their stores at the race site. Other groups and organizations would schedule bike races, dances, antique boat shows, water-skiing exhibitions,

Three members of the famed Johnson Brothers racing team receive awards at the Cambridge Yacht Club (circa 1958). The men, from left to right, are Grason Jones, Sr., Skeeter Johnson, Sidney Johnson, and Phil Johnson. The women are unidentified, but the youngster in front is Phil Johnson, who started his rookie season as an APBA driver in 1994. Photograph by Bob Layton

concerts, and marine-related arts-and-crafts exhibits to coincide with the powerboat races.

It should be noted that in these early regattas all forms of craft were entered in the races, including yachts and workboats, but these vessels were not part of the official sanctioned regatta. The sanctioning body in those days was the Maryland Power Boat Association of New York City, which was a member of the APBA. Why the Maryland Power Boat Association was located in New York City has always been somewhat of a mystery, but one theory is that it was simply an incorporated body which could obtain a quick official sanction from APBA.

Steve Sharp of Havre de Grace, Maryland, who began as a powerboat racing competitor, advanced to become an APBA official, and has come to be an interested fan, gave us a brief look at the everchanging aspects of the sport in the Chesapeake Bay region in his "Glance into the Past" article for a 1984 issue of the *HiPointer* newsletter. It is reprinted here with his permission.

> Thirty years ago our sponsors were all yacht clubs. (Maryland YC, Cambridge YC, Miles River YC, Bush River YC etc.). Each club was responsible for providing a clock, buoys, and necessary equipment. We never knew from week to week what sort of clock would be there. And buoys—they ran from cork floats to inner-tubes with a basket on top! And the President's Cup—50 gallon oil drums! If you hit one of those babies, you lost all. The inboards and outboards each had a set of ancient stop watches—always in need of repair. Al Bauer was usually our referee and announcer. He brought his own flags. We did require an ambulance and fire equipment, but the safety boat left something to be desired. We were lucky if we had a Stoke's basket. Our safety helmets were like a pot with leather ear flaps and a strap. Our safety jackets were big bulky things stuffed with kapok.
>
> If a race was blown out on Saturday, we could run Saturday and Sunday programs on Sunday. Talk about action—those crazy PODs were something else—racing runabouts, 48 runabouts, 91s, 225s, 266s. It was not unusual to have thirty 136s

> and thirty 280s entered at a race. [A POD is a Pacific One Design, which was popular in the forties. Similar to a runabout pleasure boat, it was a 14-foot single step hydroplane that used a stock Ford 60 engine. The PODs were very heavy since they were constructed of one-half-inch mahogany with an oak frame.] We did not have a High Point Dinner until 1958, when it was held at Centreville, MD. For years after Al Pierson solicited funds to put on those annual affairs at the Grasonville VFW. It was much later when the outboards joined us.
>
> In 1972 we turned the corner. As Region chairman, I instituted the region entry fees: $1.00 for outboards and $2.00 for inboards. Whew, the flack and criticism I took over that. It was the best thing we ever did. That made it possible for the region to provide first class equipment for all categories. Each category had their own clock, buoys, flags, safety equipment, trailers, etc.
>
> We used to have a one day region meeting. Most of the time was spent on ironing out racing schedules. We changed that to two days to include seminars, category meetings, etc. I also started the newsletter, which was later taken over by the Maryland Boat Racing Club.
>
> Wonder what the next 30 years will be like?"

In 1983 Baltimore *Sun* columnist Bill Tanton, writing in a different vein, lamented the changes that had taken place: "There was a time, thirty years ago or more, when Baltimore was a speedboat mecca. In a given year there were at least 10 big events held within twenty miles of City Hall—at Broening Park, on Middle River, Rock Creek, Bush River, Curtis Creek."

Essex continues to have its Governor's Cup Regatta each year at Cox's Point on the Back River. The race was initially sponsored by the Stoney Creek Racing Association and later by the Baltimore Recreation and Parks Board. It became known officially as the Governor's Cup Regatta in 1972. The Essex course is a popular course among the drivers since it is regarded as one of the fastest racecourses in the East.

Most of the other Baltimore regattas were run from the 1940s through the mid-1950s. The Maryland Yacht Club sponsored its regatta on the Patapsco River, and the course ran under the Hanover Street Bridge. The Baltimore Yacht Club held its regatta on the Middle River from about 1947 until 1952. Another popular Baltimore regatta was the Middle River Regatta sponsored by the Wilson Point Men's Club from about 1946 until 1953. The boats were launched at the Glen L. Martin plant across the river from the club, and the course included the kilo trials for straightaway records. The Stoney Creek Boat Club sponsored a race in the 1950s on Curtis Creek near the U.S. Coast Guard Station.

Al Bauer is considered by most powerboat racing authorities to be the best referee/announcer in the sport's history.

Racing events spread throughout the Chesapeake region in the middle decades of the century. In Havre de Grace races were conducted—with interruptions—from 1930 to 1990, sponsored first by the Havre de Grace Yacht Club, later by the Lions Club, and finally by the Susquehanna Optimist Club. The Miles River Yacht Club sponsored the St. Michaels powerboat regatta for many years until about 1971. The Solomons Island regatta was run on the Patuxent River until the late fifties, and the Chestertown regatta was run on the Chester River until the mid-sixties. Colonial Beach, Hopewell, and Urbanna, Virginia, also sponsored regattas in the 1950s.

Some areas were able to maintain racing enthusiasm into the eighties and nineties. The Kent Island Yacht Club sponsored the Chesapeake Bay Regatta, which was held on Hog Bay, until 1986. In 1990 the Kent Narrows Racing Association was formed and revived the race as the Kent Narrows Powerboat Challenge which also included the offshore class boats. In Hampton, Virginia, an annual powerboat regatta known as the Hampton Cup Regatta is still being run. It has become one of the major racing events on the East Coast in recent years.

The President's Cup Regatta in Washington, D.C., was one of the most hated events for the drivers. The race was run on the Potomac River at Hains Point and had a reputation for being one of the most dangerous courses in the United States. That certainly proved true in 1966 when on June 20 the phrase "Black Sunday" in relation to racing was coined. Rex Manchester, Don Wilson, and Ron Musson were all killed on the same day during the President's Cup Regatta.

The late Alton Pierson of Chester is shown here talking to fans in the pit area at Essex prior to the Governor's Cup Regatta in 1987.

The President's Cup was originally chartered by President Coolidge in 1926, and the first race was won by a gentleman named M. Gordon Hammersley in a $60,000 duraluminum craft, *Cigarette IV*. Hammersley defeated five other speedboats by averaging 52.2 miles per hour for the forty-five miles of the race. The President's Cup Regatta format changed in the mid-seventies when the unlimited hydroplanes were replaced by the Grand Prix International class. Tom "Slick" Baker of Chester, Maryland, won the 1979 President's Cup driving the *Deepwater Special* out of Ft. Lauderdale, Florida.

On April 16, 1992, *USA Today* reported:

> A Seattle group and a Washington, D.C.–area promoter hope to revive the President's Cup unlimited hydroplane race on the Potomac River between Washington and Virginia, perhaps as early as this Labor Day weekend.
>
> The race, run from 1926-79, was considered the second most important hydroplane event of the year, behind the Gold Cup.
>
> The series was dropped because of dissatisfaction with efforts to promote the race. The District's government is now trying to boost tourist interest in the nation's capital.

To my knowledge, that was the last effort to revive the President's Cup, and as of this writing there is no indication the effort has been or will be successful. Today the race sites in the Chesapeake Bay area have dwindled to five: Kent Island, Essex, and Cambridge in Maryland and Hampton and Portsmouth in Virginia.

Granddaddy of Them All: The Cambridge Regatta

To discuss the history and tradition of powerboat racing in the Chesapeake Bay region, you have to start in Cambridge, Maryland, with the granddaddy of all area powerboat regattas. There were many unofficial races on Chesapeake Bay tributaries before June 20, 1911, but on that date, the first official, sanctioned powerboat regatta was held in Cambridge. Planning actually began in February of that year, when Cambridge Yacht Club Commodore Alfred I.

DuPont named Hazelton A. Joyce, Jr., as temporary chairman of the first regatta.

A front-page story appeared in the local newspaper on June 23 with the headline, "Yacht Regatta Great Success." The writer continued: "The speed boat races were highly interesting, especially the performance of the *Sand Burr II*, a hydroplane that was sent from Atlantic City and which arrived early Tuesday morning by express. The boat, which is only 18 feet long, is equipped with a 125 horsepower engine, which drives 35 honest miles an hour. She showed the local craft what speed really is and when she slid up the river, sitting only upon her propeller, with the entire forward part of the keel out of the water, the natives wondered."

No one has ever been able to adequately explain why the folks in Cambridge are so taken by the sport of powerboat racing, but the fact remains that the powerboat regatta continues to this day. And though much has changed in the sport, the love affair between Cambridge and boat racing remains an unshakable bond. The Cambridge powerboat racing phenomenon is really a threefold relationship: the competitors, the fans, and the regatta organizers. The success of the Cambridge racers is nothing short of legendary in terms of the number of national titles, world speed records, and APBA honors they have accumulated over the past eighty-three years. The Cambridge fans are also somewhat unique in boat-racing circles in that they not only support the local regatta, but many also travel to regattas from Florida to Canada to Illinois.

Supposedly, it all started in 1909, when industrialist Alfred I. DuPont visited Cambridge aboard his yacht *Alicia* and befriended William L. Barrett and his son, Lou. DuPont was intrigued by Barrett's speedboat, which was powered by a three-horsepower, single-cylinder engine. He organized the Cambridge Yacht Club in February 1911 for the sole purpose of staging an official regatta. DuPont was no stranger to the area: He owned an estate in the Neck District and had donated prizes for a series of boat races in

The first "Classic" in Cambridge was planned aboard the steam yacht Alicia *in 1911. In June 1911, the* Sand Burr II, *owned by the White brothers of Atlantic City, New Jersey, set a world speed record for gasoline powered boats in Cambridge. Photographs courtesy of Cambridge Yacht Club.*

Cambridge for a number of years. Three days after the first official regatta was held, with rumor having it that DuPont donated $1,000 in prize money, the CYC Board of Governors decided to buy instead of lease a clubhouse.

A newspaper account described the happenings this way: "CYC, which was organized only a few weeks ago and now has a membership of over two hundred, decided that it should own instead of lease its clubhouse and at once made arrangements to purchase an old colonial home of the late Judge Charles F. Goldsborough on High St. from Mr. W. Lake Robinson." The property was described in the article as, "a mansion in perfect condition, spacious lawns, tennis courts, ample shade trees, flower beds and excellent wharfage for the yachts. It is perfectly adapted for lawn or house parties, for the house and grounds are lighted by electricity. The deal was closed at once and a payment made upon the property by its [the club's] secretary, Mr. H. A. Joyce, Jr. The purchase price was $11,500."

A second regatta was held in July of that year. The front page of the *Democrat and News* reported,

> The Cambridge Yacht Club is completing arrangements for a notable regatta to be held at Cambridge on Wednesday, July 19, 1911, when hundreds of yachts of the seven clubs of the Chesapeake Bay Yacht Racing Association will stop at Cambridge on their annual cruise. The clubs represented will be: The Capital Club of Washington, DC; The Baltimore Yacht Club, The Baltimore Motor Yacht Club, and the Corinthian Yacht Club of Baltimore; The Hampton Roads Yacht Club of Norfolk, Virginia; The Chesapeake Bay Yacht Club of Easton, and the Cambridge Yacht Club.
>
> Several hundred boats and several thousand visitors are expected. A special feature of the day will be a free-for-all motor boat race for the championship of the East, in which the fastest boats of several states will compete. One of the starters will be the *Pee Vee Ho*, owned by P. V. Hoy of Norristown, Pennsylvania. This boat is an exact duplicate of the *Sand Burr II* that created so much interest at Cambridge at the June regatta and which will race at Peoria, Illinois, next week for the National Motor Boat Championship. The *Pee Vee Ho* on the 4th of July established a world's record for speed for one mile made in competition by a 20 ft. boat. The *Pee Vee Ho* will give special exhibitions of her marvelous speed. The race will be an exciting and interesting event and worth going miles to see.

The article ended with the signatures of "James Smith, Albanus Phillips, Daniel O. Seward, V. S. Bradley—Regatta Committee."

One of the fastest early race boats from Cambridge was *Tech Jr.*, which was raced by T. Coleman DuPont. This boat set a world record in 1912 with an average speed of 58.26 miles per hour.

Of course, there has also been some negative reporting of the Cambridge regatta, as was the case in 1934. The regatta itself was staged without incident as a boat named *Man of War* dominated most of the racing, but the Associated Press also ran a sidebar story, picked up by a Baltimore paper which hit the stands the next morning with the headline, "Libelling the Choptank—Four Yachtsmen from Catonsville Claim to Have Been Driven Away by Bloodthirsty Mosquitoes."

On July 6, 1938, a new Cambridge Yacht Club was officially opened on the north side of the yacht basin—its current location on Water Street. Funds for the building were donated by Mr. and Mrs. Francis DuPont of Wilmington, Delaware, and Horn's Point (Cambridge). Mr. DuPont presented the keys of the new CYC to Commodore Carlton M. Slagle on July 4, 1938, for the club's grand opening. Emmett Andrews was regatta chairman that year, and he proudly announced on July 22: "Special attention will be given the speediest boat entered. In this race Earle W. Orem, Jr., will enter the *Seagar*. Mr. Orem's boat is capable of

Earl Orem of Cambridge shown in his 225-cubic-inch hydroplane Sea Turtle.
Photograph courtesy of Cambridge Yacht Club.

making a speed of a mile a minute and is said to exceed any boat in local waters."

In 1939 the regatta had its familiar winners such as Julius Schloss, Earl Orem, Dr. Percy Payne, Ogle Cannon, and Lou Barrett (son of William L. Barrett), but some new attractions were also a part of the festivities. The USS *Hamilton*, a Navy destroyer, and the Coast Guard vessel *Calypso* anchored for the races. Maryland's Governor O'Conor was aboard the Navy ship. WFBR radio broadcast the races live for the first time.

By 1940 the media had taken an interest in the sport, and almost all Chesapeake Bay regattas received coverage from the Baltimore *News American* and *Sun* newspapers. The *Sun* even used an airplane for the 1940 races to take special aerial photographs, which appeared in the paper's July 6, 1940, edition.

In 1948 the Cambridge Yacht Club wanted to take the regatta a step further. They announced, "A long-cherished ambition of the Cambridge Yacht Club has been to promote a Gold Cup Race. We have the facilities, including a mile and a half grandstand, 'the Choptank River Bridge.' This year come August 14th we will have a 'Gold Cup Race,' with Guy Lombardo playing host to competition in the gold cup field."

Often times today, we hear people speak about how the Gold Cup Regatta was held in Cambridge in the forties, but this is not true. The Gold Cup Regatta, first run on the Hudson River in 1904, is strictly for unlimited hydroplanes and has never been held in the Chesapeake Bay region. Nevertheless, because the unlimited hydros were added to the 1948 Cambridge regatta, it was called a "Gold Cup" race.

Guy Lombardo did indeed bring his *Temp VI* to Cambridge for the first so-called Gold Cup (unlimited) race ever held on the Choptank River. The famed orchestra leader had to settle for a second place in the race, however, as Harry Lynn of St. Louis, Missouri, took top prize in his boat *La Ha La*. That year Governor Lane presented the trophies to the winners, who included Ed

Until 1972 the pit area at Cambridge was at Long Wharf at the end of historic High Street. This aerial photograph of the pits was taken by the author about 1967.

Thompson of Dundalk in his *T.M. Special.* Carrying on a family tradition, in 1994 Ronnie Thompson, Ed's son, entered his *T.M. Special* in the Cambridge Classic.

The Gold Cup races continued to be held through 1953, but, in fact, few of the entries were true unlimited hydroplanes. Most were either 266-cubic-inch hydros or 7-liter boats. Lynn won two of the races in 1948 and 1949; Joe Van Blerck of Freeport, Long Island, captured the 1950 title; Vincent Schwing of Baltimore won in 1951; Eddie Alexanderwitz of Baltimore in his *Wee Tommy Tucker* beat out Bob Dawson of Baltimore in 1952; and Frank Foulke of Essex won the last of the Gold Cup trophies in 1953 with his *Sagana XIII.* In 1954 the Gold Cup race was changed to a free-for-all challenge in which any registered boat could enter, but there was no handicap. Bill Ritner in a boat named *Wa Wa* beat Eddie Alexanderwitz who came in second.

In 1961 the regatta format was changed to allow inboards to race on one weekend and outboards on another. Regattas had been drawing up to two hundred boats (inboards and outboards) since 1950, and the volunteer manpower was simply not sufficient to handle the logistics and problems associated with a sanctioned regatta. The pit area at Long Wharf, at the end of High Street in Cambridge, was becoming too crowded to handle all the boats and trailers, and housing accommodations were also becoming a problem.

But that is not to say the local race committee was not capable of handling its share of unforeseen problems. In 1964, for example, when Robert Wilson was regatta chairman, the wind was kicking up making the race course on the Choptank River too rough and dangerous for racing. The absolutely last thing a regatta chairman wants to do is inform people who have traveled hundreds of miles to race that the regatta is canceled. Wilson called the weather service, but received the news that no change in the weather was anticipated. He quickly gathered his race committee together and announced his decision: "All racers, hook up your boat and trailers. All regatta committee workers, gather up all the equipment and pack it up. Everybody follow me." Wilson "simply" moved the regatta from the Dorchester County side of the Choptank River to the Talbot County side in a protected area known as Bollingbrook Creek. A full race schedule was held both days in that September of 1964.

The Cambridge regatta has had its ups and downs and its joys and sorrows since that first June event of 1911. More than twenty national championships have been settled in Cambridge, and more than twenty-five approved world speed records, some dating back to 1940, have fallen on the Choptank. The regatta has also served as a stepping-stone for many competitors to further their own racing careers. While still a teenager, the late Dean Chenoweth, driver of the famed unlimited hydroplane *Miss Budweiser*, captured a national title in Cambridge in 1956. Other unlimited competitors, such as Bill Schumacher, Larry Lauterbach, Wheeler Baker, and Tom D'Eath raced in the Chesapeake Bay region before graduating to unlimited hydroplanes.

Over the years, the annual race has attracted national attention. In addition to bandleader Guy Lombardo, who drove his unlimited *Tempo VI* in the race in 1948, there was movie star Robert Mitchum, who served as race chairman in the 1960s while a CYC member. The nation's eyes were again on the Cambridge race in 1972 when the regatta was designated by the Gulf Oil Corporation as a Gulf Marine Racing Classic.

Cambridge is not the only city in the United States that shows its love of powerboat racing. The citizens of Madison, Indiana, currently have a $390,000 debt in boat racing. The individuals of this midwestern town own and operate an unlimited hydroplane named *Miss Madison*. Samuel F. DuPont donated a boat to the town many years ago, and now the thirteen thousand citizens (approximately the same number as live in Cambridge) spend approximately $435,000 a year on the unlimited race boat with an all-volunteer crew. Much as it does in the Chesapeake area, boat-racing tradition flows deep in the Ohio Valley.

The Cambridge Powerboat Regatta Association

By the 1960s, the rules of APBA were becoming far more stringent, primarily as a result of escalating insurance costs, and the demands of sponsoring a sanctioned regatta now required persons with an extensive knowledge of powerboat racing and the rules and regulations of APBA.

The Cambridge Yacht Club gave up its sponsorship of the regatta following the 1970 race, and in 1971 the Cambridge Jaycees assumed the role of sponsor. Elwood "Woody" Pliescott, Jr., who was an active Jaycee at the time, became race director, and in 1972 moved the racecourse from the Choptank River onto Hambrooks Bay. The rationale for the move was twofold. First,

Elwood "Woody" Pliescott, Jr., of Cambridge (right) is shown being inducted into the Gulf Marine Racing Hall of Fame in 1960. Courtesy of APBA.

more space was available at the new site for both the spectators and the competitors' pit area. A piece of city-owned property known as Great Marsh more than adequately served both needs. Secondly, Pliescott hoped that Hambrooks Bay would provide a better racing course, because what was known as Rooster Island would help to stop the "rollers" from pleasure boat traffic out in the Choptank from reaching the racecourse. Pliescott had a new 1⅔-mile course surveyed in the area, with most of it in Hambrooks Bay. Only a portion poked out into the Choptank River. This

The Cambridge Power Boat Regatta Association, Inc., a nonprofit organization, was organized by Ed Nabb, Skeeter Johnson, Sid Johnson, and the late Sam Cannon (seated) *to keep the powerboat racing tradition alive in Cambridge.*

course was used until 1978 when, for the first time since 1911 for a reason other than war or weather, a regatta was not scheduled in Cambridge.

Unwilling to let the tradition die, a small group of powerboat racing enthusiasts formed the Cambridge Power Boat Regatta Association, Inc., to revive the regatta and bring back a sanctioned event in 1979. Sid Johnson, longtime racer and official of APBA, was selected as chairman, and by 1980 the CPBRA had convinced fifty-six inboard drivers to return to Cambridge for racing.

I was living in Salisbury at the time, and Sid's brother Skeeter called me to join the CPBRA to assist in promoting the rebirth of the regatta. I had been on the APBA Press Advisory Committee for a number of years and had also been a sports editor at the local newspaper for seven years, from 1966 to 1972. I put together a twelve-page, photocopied program and sent out some press releases for that 1980 event.

When the big day arrived approximately five thousand spectators positioned themselves along the shoreline of Great Marsh and were treated to some victories by the hometown racers. Sid Johnson, driving his 280-cubic-inch hydroplane *Country Boy* swept both heats on Sunday while nephew Sarge won both heats of the 145-cubic-inch class with his *Sarge's Barge.* Don Craig of Salisbury won the 1200-cubic-centimeter division in the *Salisbury Stake.* The Winazak brothers, Dale and Wayne, of Salisbury placed 1-2 in the 2.5-liter modified class. Jay Wheatley's Jersey Speed Skiff *Mud Flat Missile II* of Cambridge was driven by Dave Paraskevas to a victory.

The following excerpt from a letter sent to the local newspaper illustrates the success of the return of racing to Cambridge: "The skiff drivers and riding mechanics would like to commend the efficiency of all who contributed to the smooth operation of the race. The Cambridge race is again developing into one of the high spots on our schedule. We appreciate the hospitality and special treatment we received from everyone in Cambridge. The corn-party welcome, the awards dance, the crabs—need we say more about how much we enjoyed ourselves. We're looking forward to returning next year."—Mr. and Mrs. Mark H. Outten, Oceanport, N.J.

Following the successful 1980 regatta, the CPBRA committee members discussed long-range plans, which included the possibility of a corporate sponsorship to help defray some of the regatta expenses. We thought our financial problems were solved in May of 1981 when I met with Mike Reynolds of Anheuser-Busch, Inc., out of St. Louis. We met in my home in Salisbury where I had gathered all the information I could on the history of the regatta and its unquestioned tradition. Beginning my presentation to Mr. Reynolds, I expected to have a long and arduous task before me, but within ten minutes he stopped me.

"How much money do you need?" he asked. I gave him a copy of the financial statement, and he smiled and said, "I'll have a check for you soon." I was absolutely dumbfounded. Within a few weeks, however, Mr. Reynolds called to say that Anheuser-Busch could not sponsor the regatta due to a potential beer license violation. The CPBRA had filed for a temporary license to sell beer at the regatta, and Mr. Reynolds explained that since the money was for the CPBRA, it would be against the law for his company to donate. But, he added, all we needed to do for the next year's regatta was to have an individual, or another group, apply for the beer license, and he would see that we got full sponsorship. Mr. Reynolds was promoted and relocated in the fall of that year, and the full sponsorship was never realized.

The race in Cambridge today is still sponsored by the Cambridge Power Boat Regatta Association, Inc. During a 1980 CPBRA meeting, local members voted to officially name the regatta the Cambridge Powerboat Regatta Classic; today it is generally referred to simply as The Classic.

The Cambridge Powerboat Regatta Classic

Some years ago I wrote:

> The Classic is a unique undertaking that is no small deal. And the race, or more accurately, series of races, is only part of what has become a festive weekend for thousands of people from Florida to Canada.
>
> It is a family oriented event. An annual social gathering. A reunion of sorts. More a summertime habit than anything else. The Classic weekend is an outdoor cracker barrel caucus en-

twined with, worthy of remark, a decidedly dangerous sporting event.

And the fact that The Classic remains a free admission professional sports event may also account for its popularity. A lingering wholesome appeal probably best describes The Classic's continuance.

Although the American Power Boat Association sanctioned affair is a most serious and hazardous happening, which re-

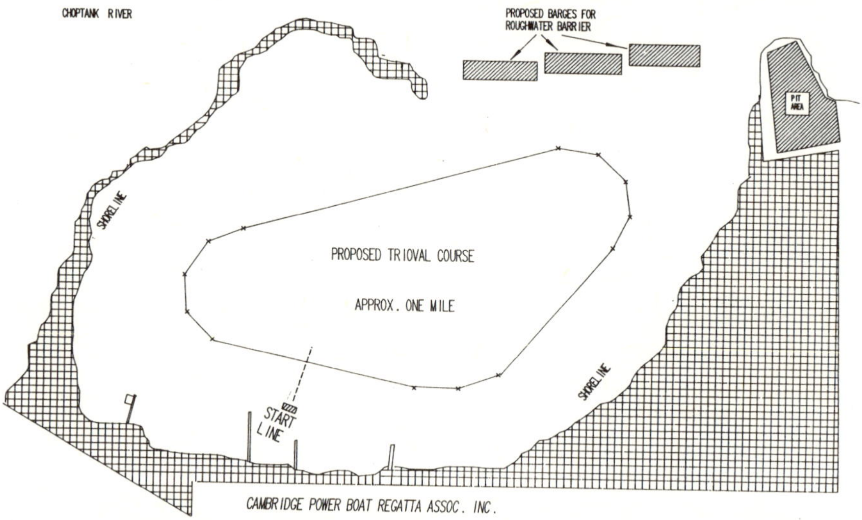

A diagram of a new one-and-a-quarter-mile course approved for records on Hambrooks Bay in Cambridge completed in 1982. The course had previously been located on the Choptank River in front of the Cambridge Yacht Club.

quires months of planning by the CPBRA, it also carries an air of serenity and unassuming, forthright friendliness. The Classic is also a combination of excitement and fun for both the racers and spectators. Cut-off jeans, no socks, and sunburn are just a few of the hallmarks of spunky little Cambridge's oldest and most famous event.

Limited powerboat racing is a forbidding sport full of folks who are restlessly brave and autonomous and like to prove it.

Former racer and APBA Region Four chairman Steve Sharp and his wife enjoy a relaxing moment before the start of a Cambridge Classic Regatta.

It is an exuberant sport brimming with racers who operate in a dangerous element for free.

The Classic is easily identified with racers devouring buttered sweet corn, crabcakes, watermelon, cantaloupe, and steamed crabs in the traditional regatta hospitality, but for those who compete or merely attend, The Classic, an event not fit to hold a candle to a Daytona 500, Indy 500, or Gold Cup, there is the obvious steely dedication and affection for the event that has been a part of Cambridge's history.

There have been times of frustration, depression, and even confidence-shaking for the local sponsoring boating group, but undaunted they keep plugging away to keep alive the oldest sanctioned professional sports event on Delmarva.

Earl Hall of Hampton, Virginia, in his 7-liter hydroplane Bluewater Special.
Photograph by Tom Kelly

George Diering of Laurel, Maryland, in his 7-liter hydroplane
Chesapeake Lady. *Photograph by Tom Kelly*

3

Battling the Wheel: Powerboat Racing Drivers

Here's one unknown author's impression of boat racing: "To see a boat race is to witness the competitive nature of mankind. A racing machine possesses a certain grandeur when hurtling down a straightaway. The sounds of a well tuned engine propelling these aquatic airplanes is in itself the echo of man's drive and desire to be the best he can. In essence, the lofty canvassed vessels of our past and the propeller driven hulls of today are the same. They are extensions of the competitive spirit in all of us."

Polly Wright

The Gulf Oil Corporation was a major sponsor of powerboat racing in the 1940s and 1950s. Shown here is the cover of the Marine Racing Review *magazine published by the Gulf Oil Corporation in 1941.*

The 1940 Gulf Marine Racing Hall of Fame inductees included Polly Wright and W. Earle Orem of Cambridge. Polly was the first woman inducted into the Hall of Fame.

A large number of drivers from the Chesapeake Bay region have possessed that competitive spirit and have earned state, national, and international recognition. In 1940, for example, W. Earle Orem, Jr., and Polly Wright, both of Cambridge, were the first two persons from the Bay area to be inducted into the Gulf Marine Racing Hall of Fame. Orem and engineman Arlington Adkins were famous for the *Sea* boats. Earle, publisher of the Cambridge *Democrat and News*, built a little 22-cubic-inch boat named *Seagar* to start his career. He also had boats named *Seagull*, *Sea Flea*, and *Sea Turtle*. In 1940 he won nineteen of twenty-one races, including victories at Lake Hopatcong, New Jersey; Cambridge; Baltimore; and Washington, D.C., in his Pacific One Design (POD) *Sea Flea*. Earle set a world speed record at Washington at 50.183 miles per hour. He was APBA Eastern Divisional champion in 1941, and in 1951 won all six races he entered.

Orem built the *Sea Turtle*, a 225-cubic-inch hydroplane, and the boat's Ford engine was built by his friend Arlie Adkins. Adkins remembers, "The *Sea Turtle* was painted aqua and the engine cover was orange, so it was a rather unique-looking boat. We tested her in 1949, but it wasn't until 1950 that the *Sea Turtle* won her first race. I think she won twenty-one races that year. When Earle raced her in Baltimore, the course was laid out under the Hanover Street bridge, and you had to go between the bridge supports on the straightaway. Earle had a poor start and he kicked her coming out of the first," Arlie said. "When he went under the bridge he was in the lead all right, but he was two pylons away from the opening he was aiming for. We never could get her to steer right."

At the St. Michaels regatta in 1951 the *Sea Turtle* struck a beer can floating in the water. Adkins recalls, "It tore a hole in her bottom eighteen inches wide and about two feet long. Earle drove her ashore into a cornfield to keep her from sinking. The can came right up through the cockpit and sailed past his head.

The most dangerous thing anybody can do is to throw something into the water during a powerboat race."

Although Arlie Adkins never made it to the Gulf Marine Racing Hall of Fame, many boat racers credit him with their success. "Without any engineering education, Arlie did things that race car builders and engineers learned to do thirty years later," said Cambridge attorney Edward Nabb, Sr. "Arlie had the idea that the motor would run faster if all the pistons, rings, and rods all weighed the same. One Sunday afternoon we borrowed the postmaster's scales from the post office and weighed everything. We took the lightest and shaved the others. Today that is called static balancing and it's pretty standard, but Arlie was doing it in 1946."

In addition to Orem and Nabb, Adkins also built engines for Elwood Pliescott and Fulton Moore. He built the engines to suit

Ed Nabb of Cambridge shown in his Pacific One Design (POD) Black Magic.
Photograph courtesy of Ed Nabb

the driver's request. "It depended on what the driver wanted," he said. "Earle Orem wasn't that concerned about a speed record. He was interested in winning races. But Fulton Moore wanted a Crosley engine that would set a world record. I told him I could build him an engine that would do it, but it wouldn't run very long," Adkins recalls with a grin. "The engine blew up the first day he raced it—right after he set the mile straightaway record."

Nabb added, "One day when I was testing my boat an exhaust stack blew off and the engine slowed down. Arlie got a hacksaw and began to saw off the exhaust stacks an inch at a time. Each time the engine ran faster, then finally it slowed down. When it slowed down, Arlie put half an inch back. Today that's called tuned exhaust, and everybody does it, but Arlie did it forty-five years ago."

In 1940 Polly Wright became the first woman elected to the Gulf Marine Racing Hall of Fame. She drove Tommy Chatfield's 91-cubic-inch hydroplane *Scoundrel* to a kilo record of 56.604 miles per hour at Havre de Grace that year. Polly, who was originally from the Philadelphia area, fell in love with the town of Cambridge while racing there and eventually made it her home. She is still a resident of the city.

In 1947 Ed Nabb entered the elite boat-racing group sponsored by the Gulf Oil Corporation. Nabb had bought one of Earl Orem's boats and named it *Black Magic*. It was a POD, and he won the eastern divisional championship with it. Nabb recalled: "It was a treacherous boat and had a habit of getting upside down. In 1947 I entered twenty-one races and won eighteen of them. I probably would have won the other three since I was in the lead every time when I turned over. The boat was designed to run about 35 miles per hour, and I was pushing her to about 50 miles per hour." *Black Magic* was a Pacific One Design (a stepped hull, not a hydroplane) and was powered by a 60-horsepower V-8 Ford engine once used in a light delivery van. "The engine was designed to run at 3,200 revolutions per minute, but when Arlie Adkins got through with it, it turned 5,000," Nabb says.

Ed, an attorney in Cambridge, was also one of the first individuals to win all three of powerboat racing's most prestigious honors. In additional to being a member of the Gulf Marine Racing Hall of Fame, he was elected to the APBA Honor Squadron and he won the UIM Medal of Honor. Ed was also the first American to head a UIM Commission; in 1970 he was named director of the UIM Offshore Commission. He still serves on the UIM commission.

In 1950 W.L. (Lou) Barrett, Jr., of Cambridge was selected to the Gulf Marine Racing Hall of Fame. He raced a boat called *Ava Lou II*. The boat, a class B racing runabout, was built by local Bill Glazier, a Philadelphia boat racer who moved to Cambridge and started a well-drilling business. Lou won thirteen of fourteen heats in 1947 and broke the class speed record three times in 1948. He sat out 1949 due to injuries, but was back in 1950 when he captured eight wins.

Ava Lou II was powered by a Ford V-8 with a 136-cubic-inch block. "You could have one carburetor for every two cylinders," remembers Arlie Adkins. "And you could use any kind of fuel you wanted—nitro, acetone, amyl-acetate. We could really make her go. Mr. Barrett, like many Cambridge racers before and after, suffered tough luck racing before his hometown fans in Cambridge. He broke his shoulder at the Cambridge race in 1949." In addition to his most successful B racing runabout, he had also raced outboards and later moved on to a hydroplane, but neither brought him the racing fame he earned in *Ava Lou*.

Elwood "Woody" Pliescott, Sr., also of Cambridge, started his racing career in 1950 with the class D racing runabout *My Boy Woody*. He set a kilo record at New Martinsville, West Virginia, in 1951 at 69.769 miles per hour. Woody won the national high point championship in 1951, was national champion in 1952, and was inducted into the Gulf Marine Racing Hall of Fame in

1953. In 1955 he built a 225-cubic-inch hydroplane and purchased an engine from famed builder Keith Black of California. Pliescott continued racing through the 1957 season, after which he retired from the sport due to increasing business demands.

Then came one of the most colorful and legendary drivers in APBA history. Calvert "Skeeter" Johnson started racing brother Sid's 136-cubic-inch hydroplane *Beverly Ann* in 1954. After much success in that boat, he signed on to race for Bill Ritner in 1961 in the cockpit of the *Wa Wa*. Skeeter captured ten APBA national championships and set no less than six world speed records. In 1968 while driving the *Miss Washington DC* on Lake Maggoire in St. Petersburg, Florida, he suffered near-fatal injuries and was hospitalized for three months. "The doctors had to rebuild my hip and arm and during my rehabilitation I thought I would lose everything I had to pay the medical expenses. The Kent Island Yacht Club organized a benefit party for me in 1968. That just tore me up. There I was, down and out, and my boat-racing friends and family gave me strength and financial support while I got better."

Calvert "Skeeter" Johnson of Cambridge shown in Bill Ritner's 266-cubic-inch hydroplane Wa Wa.

Skeeter retired from racing until 1972 when a friend, Tony Scartine, asked him to drive his new 280-cubic-inch hydroplane *First State*. Skeeter drove the boat that year and won another national title at Miami, Florida. He then retired for good after twenty-eight years of racing. His Gulf Marine Racing Hall of Fame induction came in 1956. Skeeter Johnson was later inducted into the APBA Honor Squadron (1969) and the State of Maryland Athletic Hall of Fame (1984).

He says there is nothing he would rather do today than to be able to climb back into the cockpit of a hydroplane and go racing. "It's something that gets in your blood," he says. "I miss the people more than anything. Boat-racing people are like family. They're very close. Of course a lot of my friends in boat racing are dead—killed by the boat. But when you're young, you don't have fear." In 1967 Skeeter Johnson was offered the job of driving the unlimited hydroplane *Miss Budweiser*. "I turned down the Bud deal because I knew it would keep me away from my family a lot. I often thought about that decision though," he adds. "I imagine if I had done it, I would have liked it and probably would have ended up dead, like so many of them. You have to be a little crazy

Elwood "Woody" Pliescott, Jr., of Cambridge gives a wave as he passes committee boat in his 150-cubic-inch hydroplane Woody Jr.'s Special.

to drive a race boat." Today, Skeeter faces an even tougher challenge related to the sport. His son, Phil, entered the dangerous field of powerboat racing in 1994, keeping alive a fifty-year-old family tradition, and Skeeter watches helplessly from the shoreline.

In 1960 Elwood "Woody" Pliescott, Jr., continued in the family tradition and joined his father in the Gulf Marine Racing Hall of Fame. Woody dominated the 150-cubic-inch class for a decade with his Lauderbach hull and Keith Black–prepared engines in a boat named *Woody Jr.'s Special.* He entered the 100 miles per hour club in 1963 and captured several APBA national championships. In 1965, 1966, and 1968, he won the national high point title. Pliescott was also APBA eastern divisional champion from 1965 through 1968.

Woody, Jr., briefly retired from active racing in 1969, but kept active in the sport as an engine builder. "Tom D'Eath wanted me to build him an engine," Pliescott recalls, with a chuckle. "Since he couldn't beat me on the racecourse, he thought this was a good way for me to make him a winner." The Pliescott-D'Eath partnership produced a hydroplane named *Southern Style*, powered by a slant-six Plymouth engine, that set a world straightaway record of 126 miles per hour—11 miles per hour faster than the previous mark. The partnership also brought a 1970 APBA national championship.

In 1973 Pliescott ordered a new Ron Jones–built hydro and named it *Family Affair*. It was another 150-cubic-inch-class boat, and he had built his own engine. "The hull was really experimental," he says. It was powered by an outdrive [an inboard engine with an outboard propulsion system]. The boat was controversial, but not a winner. It went through a turn real good, but it wouldn't go very fast in a straight line. In 1974 we went back to a conventional drive. That year we set a world record of 88 miles per hour on Labor Day and that record stood for fourteen years." Pliescott retired for good in 1976.

The last Cambridge inductee into the Gulf Marine Racing Hall of Fame was George Cusick in 1961. He started his racing career at age thirty-one running his own 136-cubic-inch hydroplane, *Scared Rabbit.* Cusick signed on with Bob Tuttle of Northport, Long Island, in 1960 to drive a new Harold Ruark–built hull *Red Top.* The partnership proved successful, and the *Red Top* team was a dominant force in the 145-cubic-inch class. George won four national championships and five high point titles in *Red Top.* He also captured a national title in 1967 driving Steve Sharp's *Bonanza* in Guntersville, Alabama. George was named *Popular Boating*'s "Driver of the Year" in 1962.

According to Cusick he took up powerboat racing to relax. "My doctor told me I needed to relax more and suggested I get a hobby," he recalls. "I didn't have money enough for a really fast boat until Bob called me saying he was looking for a driver. That deal worked out pretty good for both of us. I knew the boat would be good because it was built by Harold Ruark in Cambridge. We had a V-8 Ford 136-cubic-inch flat-head engine and later we put in a Ford Falcon straight-six with 140 cubic inches. Cusick says the good times of boat racing outweigh the bad. "I had two accidents: one at St. Michaels and one at Red Bank, New Jersey. They weren't serious at the time, but I feel it now. But there were a lot of good times. I

George Cusick

loved everything about racing, except the trips back home."

Cusick is a retired automobile technician, but still helps out young boat racers. He continues to be a member of the Cambridge Power Boat Regatta Association and works on engines for racers Jim Ruark and Dave Bromwell. In 1991, Cusick was inducted into the State of Maryland Athletic Hall of Fame.

Frankie Foulke of Essex was inducted into the APBA Honor Squadron in 1961. Frank had first become involved in powerboat racing in 1939 when he built his first motor. Over the next twenty years or so, he went on to set twenty-eight speed records while racing in all inboard classes. Frank was also inducted into the Gulf Marine Racing Hall of Fame and was a member of the 100 miles per hour club. He later served as chairman of various APBA inboard technical committees and was inboard vice-president.

Another Cambridge driver, Robert "Barge" Bromwell, race director of The Classic for an unprecedented eight years from 1983 to 1990, came close to election to the APBA Hall of Champions in both 1986 and 1988. In 1986, Bromwell, along with stepdaughter Kim Corbman, journeyed to Lowell, Oregon, with their Jersey Speed Skiff *Together Again* and captured the APBA national championship. That year he also won the John Bramble Memorial Trophy given by APBA Region Four and the Al Bauer Memorial Award given by Regions Three and Four. He recorded other impressive victories at the Spirit of Detroit Regatta and the River Spectacular Regatta in Philadelphia. The main criteria taken into account for induction into the hall are winning the national championship and setting a world speed record; in 1986 Bromwell missed only the record.

"Barge" raced for fifteen years, winning three North American titles and five national high point crowns. He capped his career with Dave Paraskevas at the helm setting a world speed record in Portsmouth, Virginia, in 1990.

Today Cambridge has fifteen licensed drivers still competing on the APBA circuit. Grason Jones is a four-time national cham-

Robert Bromwell and Tommy Thompson of Cambridge shown in the Jersey Speed Skiff Together Again *on a trial run. Note Bromwell checking his stopwatch.*

pion in the 6-liter hydroplane class with his *Heartbreaker*; Tom and Tommy Thompson have won four consecutive Jersey Speed Skiff national titles in *The Gambler*; Jim Ruark, son of famed boat builder Harold Ruark, has a triple crown (U.S. national, Canadian national, and world championships) to his credit with his 2.5-liter stock hydroplane *Sweet Eileen*; Gee McClain holds a world speed record in the pro stock class with John Kiley's *Sweet Caroline* and has won several national titles in the super stock class with his own *April*; Sarge Johnson set a five-mile competition record in his 7-liter hydroplane *Sarge's Barge* in Cambridge a few years ago; and Tom Ruark, Lee Gore, Allen Nelson, Dale Winazak, Phil Johnson, Dave Bromwell, Jr., Bobby Brown, and George Applegate all still compete from Florida to Canada under the Cambridge flag.

Tom Thompson of Cambridge waits for the five-minute gun for the next heat of racing. Thompson and rider Ken McMullen of Annapolis captured the 1993 championship in the Jersey Speed Skiff class.

Bobby Brown completed a banner year in 1994 with his hydroplane *Catch 22*. The ten-year-powerboat-racing veteran won the national championship in the 2.5-liter stock class and was named APBA Region Four "Man of the Year." Bob, the son of another former racer—Bob, Sr.—drives two hydros on the circuit each year. In addition to his own *Catch 22*, he also competes in the 5-liter hydroplane class with John Savage's *Cloud Nine*. He also won the Stan Jones Memorial Trophy, sponsored by CPBRA, at the Cambridge Classic in 1992 and captured the North American championship that same year.

A member of a Kent Island family of race boat drivers, Wheeler Baker is one of the most successful and versatile drivers in the history of the sport, a fact not widely known in his home state at one time. Baltimore *Evening Sun* columnist, Bill Tanton, noted the fact in a 1983 column, which began with the headline, "Maryland World Record Holder Living in Anonymity in Chester."

"They were holding the first tailgating party in the history of the Maryland State Hall of Fame's induction luncheons," Tanton reported, referring to the large contingent of Kent Islanders who arrived early for the induction ceremonies of the State of Maryland Athletic Hall of Fame to honor Alton Pierson. Tanton learned from

Grason Jones of Cambridge shown in his 6-liter hydroplane Heartbreaker.

Pierson that Wheeler Baker had recently set a new world speed record. Baker was "the new owner of the world's record for seven-liter hydroplanes," wrote Tanton, commenting to Baker, "I must have missed it in the papers."

"It wasn't in any papers up here," Baker said. "The papers up here cover the Daytona 500 in detail. There are no Marylanders in that. But a Marylander sets a record in a boat race and nobody prints it."

"The man has a point," was Tanton's cryptic comment.

Wheeler started racing in 1957 as a young boy in the JU outboard division and continued up the ladder. By 1988 he had driven every type of race boat except one, had driven in as many as five classes at one regatta, had won several national and high point titles, and had set speed records.

Then in 1988 the Chester resident finally earned his due, fulfilling two dreams in the same year. Wheeler, who was forty-one

Wheeler Baker of Chester in the cockpit of his 7-liter hydroplane Baker's Dozen.

years old at the time, had won seven of eight races, the national high point title, the national championship, and the eastern divisional championship in both the 7-liter and 2.5-liter stock classes; and had set a speed record of 117.058 miles per hour at Essex. At the end of the 1987 racing season, I was still doing some sports writing, and I had written a piece endorsing Baker for the APBA Hall of Champions: ". . . despite the truckload of trophies and reams of accolades garnered during the past 10 years of competition in this exceedingly dangerous sport, the Queen Anne's County Commissioner has yet to succeed in being elected to the APBA Hall of Champions. Racing fans may find that fact rather incredible considering Baker's accomplishments in the 145-cubic-inch and 280-cubic-inch inboard classes as well as currently in the Formula MerCruiser 7-liter hydroplane class. But for Wheeler Baker the 1987 APBA racing season has been special. And it should end with a very special crowning touch. Very special indeed."

And it did. On February 13, 1988, in Ontario, California, "The Wheel" was inducted into the APBA Hall of Champions. Within a month of his induction I wrote, "Wheeler Baker will be in the cockpit of a new Jon Staudacher hull this year making him the first Eastern Shore native to ever race a thunderboat on the American Power Boat Association circuit."

Under the sponsorship of Stroh Brewery Company and Ford Motor Company, Wheeler Baker piloted the unlimited hydroplane *Miss Stroh's* and could finally say he had driven every inboard class of boat in the APBA. Today he is back to limited inboard racing and still setting speed records.

On May 14, 1988, the Kent Island Yacht Club sponsored "A Salute to Wheeler Baker" night and all of Kent Island was there. Without doubt, 1988 was a good year for the Bakers.

Also that year, Wheeler's brother Tom took over the 7-liter duties as well as continuing to race in the Grand Prix division.

The Baker Family and Alton Pierson (seated right)

Tom won the eastern division title at Raleigh, North Carolina, and set a speed record of 112.100 miles per hour in Alan Vordermeier's *Miss Stroh's Beer* at St. Petersburg, Florida. Tom has twenty-five years of racing experience in just about every class of boat. He recorded over 125 victories including the 1980 Grand Prix class championship and 5-liter and 7-liter high point titles. He posted a 1992 victory at New Brunswick, Canada, won four out of nine qualifying heats, set three course speed records, and had the fastest lap time at four events.

The Baker family continues to carry on the racing tradition with Wheeler and Tom still active racers. And in 1993, Wheeler's daughter, Gideon, started her rookie season in the 1-liter stock division. Another brother, Ted, has retired from the sport.

Alton C. Pierson was a racing legend on Kent Island, which has plenty of boat-racing history of its own. He started his career in 1956 and soon received sponsorship from his employer, R. B. Baker and Sons in Queenstown. Alton won national titles in both the 136- and 280-cubic-inch classes. He also set speed records in both classes. Alton, a member of the Gulf Marine Racing Hall of Fame, was named *Popular Boating*'s "Driver of the Year" in 1958. He was elected to the State of Maryland Athletic Hall of Fame in 1983, to *Yachting* magazine's all-American racing team and to *Motorboating* magazine's "Who's Who in Racing." Alton's boat-racing career ended in February of 1960 in St. Petersburg, Florida, when he suffered a broken leg and facial injuries at the Southland Sweepstakes Regatta.

Another famed builder/driver from Kent Island was Lem Thompson of Chester. Lem earned most of his driving fame with the 145-cubic-inch *Sandy K.* After many years of driving and winning he suffered serious injuries on July 25, 1970, at Ypsilanti, Michigan, during the national championship regatta.

Kent Island is also the home of Chris Yewell and Alan Wicker, current licensed drivers, as well as veteran Larry Lauterbach who spends most of his time today building and repairing hydroplanes instead of racing them. Lauterbach comes from a famed family of race boat builders. His father, Henry, started the family business in 1947 in Virginia. Lauterbach Custom Boats has since become one of the world's primary manufacturers, having built 250 hydroplanes.

Larry was an outstanding driver, as his five-time-national-champion status indicates. He also won twenty-six Grand Prix events and set five UIM speed records. Larry raced in every class from the smallest to the unlimiteds (in which he piloted both the *Miss Budweiser* and the *Winston Eagle*). He was inducted into the APBA Hall of Champions in 1980.

Edmund Thompson, Jr., of Baltimore is another famed driver from the Chesapeake Bay area. He began his boat-racing career in 1947 and was most famous for his *T.M. Special* boats. He set five world speed records in the years between 1948 and 1954. Ed didn't favor any specific course for his feats; he included Middle River (1948) and Bush River (1950 and 1954) for three of his record-setting runs. He also topped speed marks at New Martins-

Stu Shane of Havre de Grace in his 145-cubic-inch hydroplane HiJacker. *Photograph by Tom Kelly*

ville, West Virginia. He won twenty-seven consecutive races in 1949 and was inducted into the Gulf Marine Racing Hall of Fame that year. In 1984, Ed was selected for the Greater Dundalk Sports Hall of Fame.

Other Chesapeake Bay region drivers still active on the APBA circuit include George Applegate of Tasley, Virginia; Steve Barrett of Pasadena, Maryland; Dave Bromwell, Jr., Phil Johnson, Grason Jones, Tom Ruark, and Allen Nelson of Cambridge, Maryland; Terry McArdle of Arnold, Maryland; Keith and Ken McMullen of Edgewater, Maryland; Chuck Miller of Queen Anne, Maryland; Chris Oliver of Annapolis, Maryland; Steve Schloss of Hampton, Virginia; Stu Shane of Havre de Grace, Maryland; Bob Shukert of Severna Park, Maryland; Dale Winazak of Salisbury, Maryland; Ron Thompson of Joppa, Maryland; and Greg Williams of White Marsh, Maryland.

Chesapeake Racing Families

Powerboat racing tends to run in families in the Chesapeake Bay region. Probably the two most famous powerboat racing families on the Bay are the Johnsons of Cambridge and the Bakers of Kent Island. The Baker family, as described in an earlier section of this book, has had four members who have pursued boat-racing fame: Wheeler, his brothers Ted and Tom, and his daughter Gideon.

The Johnsons got their start into boat-racing history when Sid Johnson started out in the sport in 1945 at age nineteen as a driver; today he is still active in the sport as a race boat owner and APBA official. He and his brothers, Skeeter, Phil, and Sarge, formed the Johnson Brothers racing team and enjoyed success with the *Beverly Ann* boats for over twenty years in both the 145- and 280-cubic-inch classes. They chalked up seven world speed records and four national championships. During the Johnson Brothers' heyday, Sid was the owner and mechanic; Phil and

Tom Baker of Chester prepares to take the 7-liter hydroplane Baker's Dozen *on the Back River.*

Sarge handled the business end of the sport; and Skeeter was the driver.

Sarge, Jr., started racing a 145-cubic-inch hydro in 1979 prior to moving up to the 7-liter class with a boat named *Sarge's Barge*. In 1994 the family tradition continued when Skeeter's son Phil bought a 5-liter hydroplane and earned his APBA driver's license. After his required last place finish for a rookie driver in his first race, Phil went on to have several top five finishes in his first season as a driver.

As previously mentioned, the Johnsons, the Lauterbachs, and the Bakers are all respected names in the sport of powerboat racing, but there are other Chesapeake Bay area families who are also quite notable. The McMullens of Annapolis have been involved in the sport in various roles for many years. Nancy McMullen has served in a number of capacities for Region Four

Sarge Johnson of Cambridge checks his 7-liter hydroplane Sarge's Barge *prior to a race. Sarge is one of over twenty-five racers who have set an official speed record at Cambridge.*

and is currently APBA chief timer for the region. Pattie McMullen is the region's chief scorer, and Ken has both a driver's license and is an approved APBA referee. Ken is also the rider with Tom Thompson in the Jersey Speed Skiff *The Gambler* and drives a 1-liter hydroplane. Keith McMullen is a licensed driver and pilots two boats: his own 1-liter *Miss Gunsmoke* and a 5-liter named *Plumber's Friend.*

Charlie Miller, Sr., and son Chuck of Annapolis have also been active in the sport for many years. Charlie, Sr., now retired from active racing, used to run a 150-cubic-inch hydroplane named *Dixie Boy II*, but is more famous for his 2.5-liter *Whoopee.* Chuck, still an active racer, kept his father's boat name, driving the new *Whoopee*, which is a 2.5-liter modified.

Harold Ruark of Cambridge earned fame as a boatbuilder, but his two sons and a daughter are more renown as competitors.

Both Jim and Tom are current active racers, but daughter Connie has retired from the sport.

Although not Chesapeake Bay area natives, the Kennedy family out of Bear, Delaware, have been strong supporters of Bay races for over twenty years. George Kennedy, Sr., and wife Barbara used to race a Jersey Speed Skiff, and now son George, Jr., and daughter Patti are active as drivers. George, Jr., has raced almost every class of hydroplane and earned his share of awards along the way. He will enter a new stage in 1995, having been named driver of the Grand Prix hydroplane *Medical Systems*, and will also follow in the family tradition with his own Jersey Speed Skiff. Patti Kennedy was a successful 1-liter and 2.5-liter modified driver in the *Pop-A-Top* boats.

Racing as Equals

A unique aspect of powerboat racing has been that gender identity and equality have never been an issue in the sport. Whether one is male or female has no bearing on acceptance or degree of success. There are no special rules with respect to gender, no separate sanctioning bodies, no special equipment, and no difference in course size or shape. The rules of powerboat racing are the same for all, or in a word—equal. Women in powerboat racing are a select group of athletes who compete head to head with their male counterparts and are grouped together only as professional race drivers.

A few early female drivers earned fame on a national level. W. J. Conners, wife of a Buffalo publisher and politician, drove the *Miss Okeechobee*. The boat, built by Gar Wood, was powered by a 500-horsepower Liberty engine. She won sixty-four races during a five-year period. Helen Hentschel of Flushing, New York, raced outboards and in 1927 was high point champion. Loretta Turnbull raced a boat named *Sunkist Kid* after starting racing outboards in her native California, and Delphine Dodge Baker, who

Bobby Brown of Parsonsburg (S-22) in his 2.5-liter stock hydroplane Catch 22 *leads Ann Fitzgerald in the* Thumann's Deli Special *(S-90) through a turn. Photograph by Tom Kelly*

drove the *Miss Syndicate*, won the President's Cup in a boat powered by a 600-horsepower Packard engine.

On the Chesapeake, as mentioned earlier, Polly Wright of Cambridge was the first woman elected to the Gulf Marine Racing Hall of Fame. She drove Tommy Chatfield's 91-cubic-inch hydroplane *Scoundrel* to a kilo record of 56.604 miles per hour at Havre de Grace.

In addition to Polly, there are other Chesapeake Bay women who have achieved success in the sport. In 1939, Dorothy Twilley, daughter of Mr. and Mrs. C. Merritt Twilley of Salisbury, started competing as a fourteen-year-old. Twilley raced her father's boat, *Miss St. Paul*, at the President's Cup Regatta in Washington, D.C.,

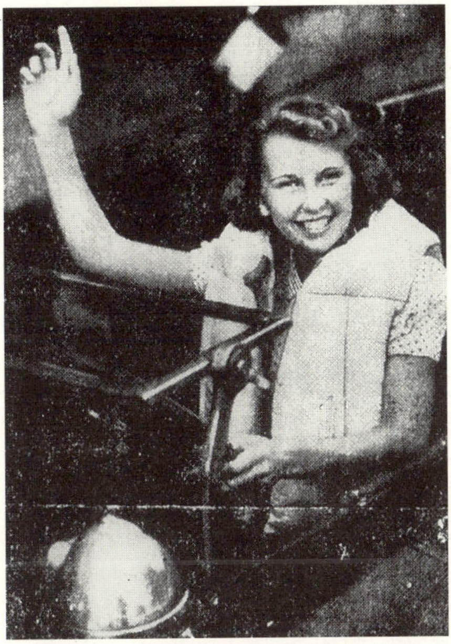

Dorothy Merritt Twilley, at age fourteen, was the youngest female competitor at the President's Cup Regatta in Washington, D.C., in 1939.

after winning races at St. Michaels and Havre de Grace. She was a member of the Maryland Yacht Club.

There was also Mildred "Millie" Foulke of Essex. Millie was the first woman to drive a speedboat in excess of 100 miles per hour. Wife of famed racer Frank Foulke, Millie recorded her feat on December 26, 1953, at the Orange Bowl Regatta in Miami, Florida. She drove her husband's 266-cubic-inch hydroplane *Sagana XIII* at an average speed of 111.289 miles per hour.

Connie Ruark and Kim Corbman, both of Cambridge, were riding mechanics in the Jersey Speed Skiff class during the eighties. Ruark rode with her brother Tom in the skiff named *Purple Haze*, and Corbman was the copilot for her stepfather, Robert Bromwell, in both the *Flip Flop* and *Together Again*. Kim rode with Bromwell for the national championship at Eugene, Oregon, in 1986 and was also credited with nine national high point championships.

Patti Kennedy of Bear, Delaware, is still active on the boat-racing scene after twenty-five years of experience. Her mother, Barbara, was also a successful driver in both the 2.5-liter stock class and Jersey Speed Skiffs.

Valerie Schloss of Prince George, Virginia, still drives a 1-liter stock hydroplane named the *Jitterbug*, owned by Roger Martin, after many years in her own hull she called the *Pink Panther*.

Slices of Life

There is unparalleled camaraderie among powerboat racers, despite the fact they are fierce competitors on the racecourse. That aspect of the sport has held true since its beginning. Never was it put to a greater test than in 1955 in the midst of the Bush River Regatta in Baltimore.

In November 1955, Elwood Pliescott, Sr., was awarded a special trophy by the American Power Boat Association for "Most Outstanding Good Sportsmanship and Heroic Deeds in the Sport." The award was a result of Pliescott's actions in August of that year at the Bush River Regatta. It was the second heat of the 225-cubic-inch hydro race. Pliescott in his boat, *My Boy Woody*, was holding a slight lead over Bill Ritner when he saw Ritner's boat *Wa Wa* nose violently into the water. Pliescott had completed the turn when he saw that a piece of Ritner's driving suit was caught on the hull of his sinking boat. Unaware that Ritner was unconscious, Pliescott turned back, shut his boat down, and leaped into the water. He successfully unhooked his friend from the hull as it went to the bottom and waited for a patrol boat to pick him up. Although Bill Ritner was injured that day, his life was saved by Elwood Pliescott.

In honor of Pliescott's unselfish act, the plaque read, "The truest measure of good sportsmanship is the Golden Rule, Matthew VII, 12; 'Therefore in ALL things, Whatsoever you would that men should do unto you, do ye even so unto them likewise.' The winner of this award is selected from worthy candidates who apply the Golden Rule to powerboat racing by: Devotion to honest rivalry, courteous relations, selfless consideration, graceful acceptance of results."

Every driver has a tale to tell of mishaps and close calls. On two occasions Gee McClain of Cambridge was thrown from his super stock *April* during a race, but with vastly different results. In June of 1980 at the Tar Heel Regatta in Raleigh, North Carolina,

Gee McClain of Cambridge puts on his driver suit preparing for a race in Cambridge. McClain is the current pro-stock speed record holder at 101.129 miles per hour for the five-mile heat. Photograph by Joey Gardner

he was into the final turn of his first lap when his boat began bouncing and became airborne. It rolled into the water sideways, throwing McClain out. He swam to a patrol boat, but the deadweight throttle on his boat failed. The boat continued winding around Lake Wheeler and eventually crashed into rocks on the other side of the inpoundment. The crowd of approximately five thousand spectators was brought to its feet as the boat went airborne, but then chuckled at the driverless boat as it ran around the lake. McClain, who was uninjured, wasn't chuckling at all. He was angry that the patrol boats didn't head off his racer and estimated it cost him about $3,000 to make repairs.

A decade later, McClain was racing in the national championship regatta at Meridian, Mississippi, when once again he was jettisoned from the cockpit of his super stock. This time, however, the boat was destroyed and the popular Cambridge driver spent a month in a Mississippi hospital.

In August 1957 some of the reality of the life of powerboat drivers was brought home to Cambridge. The Choptank River was the host of the 136-cubic-inch and 280-cubic-inch national championships that year, as well as the eastern divisional championships for the 225-cubic-inch class. Several Chesapeake Bay racers had pretty good days. Alton Pierson of Queenstown finished second in the 136-cubic-inch race; Elwood Pliescott won

Don Dunnington of Bethesda, Maryland, in his 7-liter hydroplane Maryland Miss *at Millville, New Jersey, in 1971. Photograph by Tom Kelly.*

the 225 class with his *Woody's Special*, and Don Dunnington of Bethesda finished second; Watson Lewis of Baltimore took third in the 266 division with his *We Go Too*, and Eddie Alexanderwitz won the free-for-all race. But it was Jack Casson of Oceanside, California, who got the headlines the next day. Casson drove seventy-one hours from California to compete in the 280 nationals. He had a strong fourth-place finish in the first heat, but flipped his boat in the second. He was unhurt and, after retrieving his boat, hooked it to the back of his car and drove seventy-one hours back to California. The name of his boat was *Wrecker II*.

Aside from the national titles, national high point championships, and world speed records that he won, one of Golden Hill native George Cusick's most vivid memories is of the 1961 national championship that got away. "After we had made some test runs for the nationals in San Diego we stored the *Red Top* at its trailer for the first elimination heat the next day," he remembers. Even though the practice runs had been perfect, during the first heat, the craft refused to go more than 30 miles per hour. Cusick finished in ninth place. "I was thinking, 'we drove all the way to California to finish ninth. That's terrible.' " That night the crew probed further and discovered a wad of tinfoil shoved into a gas line connected to the carburetor. "We never left the boat alone again," said George of the lesson learned that day. He came back to finish second overall after winning the final heat.

And I learned as a member of the 1968 APBA Press Advisory Board that journalists are not immune to the pranks and pitfalls associated with the sport of powerboat racing. That year, I drove, at my own expense and on my vacation days, to Guntersville, Alabama, to cover the national championship regatta. Upon arrival I learned my reservation had been lost or not recorded, and I had to drive another sixty miles to get a room. On my return trip to Cambridge I stopped for dinner and my car was broken into and everything stolen (even my dirty laundry). My worse fear was what reaction would my publisher display when he learned

A young John Loller of Baltimore appears snug in the cockpit of his 1200cc hydro Bounty Hunter. *Photograph by Tom Kelly*

that his expensive camera was gone and that I had absolutely nothing to show for my trip other than what I could remember. He took it rather well at first, but later questioned my account of what happened. He said he had received information that I had sold the camera in Guntersville to garner enough money to try to win favors with the regatta queen. I later learned the information was offered by none other than prankster George Cusick.

4

Behind the Scenes: The Hidden Heroes

The sport of powerboat racing, like all sports, has changed dramatically since its beginnings. In the early days of racing, most competitors built their own boats, painted them, stuck an engine in them, and went racing. For example, in 1938, Earle Orem built his 225-cubic-inch hydroplane *Seagar* in his spare time on the second floor of his father's publishing house on High Street in Cambridge.

The research and development aspect of the sport was done during competition. Ed Nabb once told me that when he first started racing with Orem there were two persons in the boat: the driver and a mechanic. The mechanic had a couple of duties, including pumping gas into the engine (the boats did not have fuel pumps) and keeping track of the number of laps. This was done by placing adhesive tape strips on the dashboard and peeling one off each time a lap was completed.

Today, from the drawing board to the racecourse is a long and laborious period. Boatbuilding is now a science as well as an art, and there are few competitors left who could build their own race boats. Two of the most famous builders today are Ron Jones of California and Jon Staudacher of Michigan, but the Bay region is not without its famed craftsmen.

On the Bay, Harold Ruark of Cambridge built several national champion hulls in the thirty years that he crafted limited inboard hydroplanes. A self-taught engineer, he has traced the evolution from flat-bottom boats to the true hydroplane or three-pointer, with its two sponsons and a fraction of the propeller skimming the water.

All of Harold's boats until the mid-1980s were of a conventional nature, with the engine placed in front of the driver, as

A rare photograph of Skeeter Johnson piloting the 150-cubic-inch Chromium *gives an illustration of the "prop-rider" effect. Photograph by Bobby Layton.*

opposed to the current cab-over design in which the engine is moved back and the driver is in front. Many thought that the location of the driver prompted the design change.

"Not so," said Harold. "It really doesn't matter where the person sits, up front or in back of the engine. Where the difference in the construction comes in is under the boat. They [cab-over hulls] have real wide transoms to keep the boat up, which is probably so assuming the rpms of the engine are also up.

"I remember Henry Lauterbach and I were up in Michigan at the nationals one year and we were listening to this announcer go on about this stuff of how the cab-overs from California were going to blow everybody else away. Well, Charlie Dunn was driving the *Miss Washington, DC* and boy did he put it on those guys from the West Coast in their cab-overs. I mean he beat the hide off those boys. Henry turned to me and said in that broken German accent of his, 'The boat don't know where the guy is sitting.' "

Harold does concede that another change in design has proven beneficial. "The smartest thing they did was when they made these pickle-fork hulls. They cut away all that unnecessary area up front on the bow and distributed the weight properly."

He goes on to point out how important aerodynamics have become in raceboat construction. The hull must be designed so that air pressure on top of a curved front deck keeps the boat down, while air pressure in a tunnel between the sponsons lifts it up. When designed and built correctly, one compensates for the other in a properly balanced race boat. As the boat rises on a column of air, it "walks" from sponson to sponson, barely touching the water.

As with design and aerodynamics, the materials used in race boats have also changed. Harold Ruark's early boats were built primarily of quarter-inch plywood. Now builders are using lighter and stronger materials, such as fiberglass and Kevlar. One of Harold's most recent boats, currently the *My Girl* owned by Dave Bromwell, is primarily a wooden hull with a fiberglass cockpit and

Sid Johnson of Cambridge in his 5-liter hydroplane Beverly Ann *holds a slim lead over the* Encore II. *Photograph by Tom Kelly.*

engine cowling topping off the Sitka spruce and plywood design. The big difference, he said, is in the glues used to hold the hulls together. "Today's epoxies are so much better and stronger," said Ruark. "And creating a winning design is a matter of trial and error and experience. You think you have it right, but then it's not by a long shot. You bring it in, redo what you have or start over. Sometimes it is better to scrap it and start from scratch."

He remembers the first race boat he ever built, an outboard runabout, twelve feet long. He sold it to someone to play around in, literally giving it away. "It wasn't worth a nickle," he said.

Harold's list of famed boats includes seven national championship hulls. He built two *Beverly Ann*s for the Johnson Brothers Racing team of Cambridge; two *Lil Barb*s for R.B. Baker and driver Alton Pierson of Queenstown; three *Red Top*s for Bob Tuttle and driver George Cusick of Cambridge; and the *Lil Lectron* for Willard Wilson of Wilmington, Delaware. The *Budget Buster*, built for owner/driver Ray Lynn of Philadelphia in 1972, was supposed to have been his last hull design, but thirteen years later, his son Jimmy asked him to build one more racing hydroplane. So in 1985 Harold Ruark went back to his shop and built a 2.5-liter stock hydroplane—a cab-over design at that.

That boat also brought famed driver George Cusick out of retirement. Some racers retire from the cockpit and become active as officials, volunteers, or crew chiefs. Some become mechanics. George Cusick falls into the category of driver-to-mechanic. Since his retirement in 1970, the Golden Hill native has been to only one powerboat event. He still hears the roaring engines of the Cambridge Classic from his home though. "I feel like when you quit, then you quit," he said. "I stayed away to keep from getting the itch."

In 1985, however, Harold Ruark convinced George to build the engine for his son Jimmy's 2.5-liter stock hydroplane, the

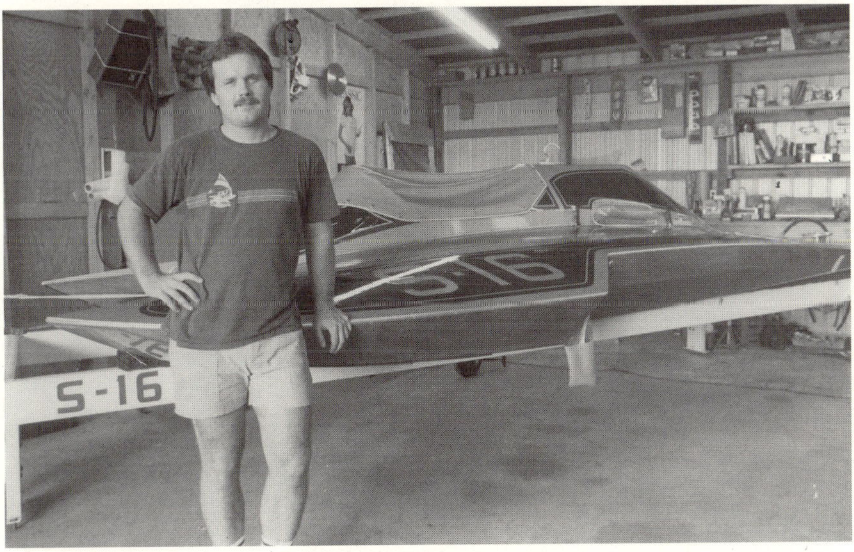

Jimmy Ruark of Salisbury stands in his father's shop by his 145-cubic-inch hydroplane Sweet Eileen.

Sweet Eileen. "We'd been friends for years," said George. "He talked me into it. I'm not really that good, and the engines today are altogether different from when I raced." Work once done by hand, such as a valve job, is now done in a machine shop, he added, noting that the modern 2.5-liter hydros use a modified Ford Pinto engine, instead of the small, 60-horsepower, V-8 engine, known as a "Flathead Ford," with which he set his speed records. Also, said George, being a mechanic has its pitfalls, like "working all night and all that kind of stuff."

Two years later Jimmy drove the *Sweet Eileen* to a national championship at Miami, Florida, and in 1988 won the world championship in Valleyfield, Canada.

An indication of how different it is today is that you can actually buy race boat kits. The design, construction, welding, hardware installation, and machine work are done at a shop. A buyer simply orders the boat. The kit boat can even be specialized with such features as custom-built sponsons.

Many factors affect the success of a race boat. Today, most competitors have several propellers or wheels of varying sizes and pitch. Most engines are "stock" automotive engines, but they need to be modified and reworked to perform properly in a boat. The economic status of a particular racer determines how much work will be done on his or her engine and who will do it. There are plenty of specialized racing engine builders in business who charge a rather substantial price, which some racers can afford. Others prefer to tinker with their own engines.

According to Ed Nabb, it is quite different today from when he started racing in 1938. Research and development were done during competition back then. Techniques such as "tuning an exhaust" and "static balancing," as described in an earlier chapter, were discovered as a result of drivers and mechanics applying trial and error methods in the early days of racing. "But, there are still a few boat racers today that approach the sport as we did," says Nabb. "They tinker with their boats and engines in their garage with the help of family and friends. And they know it would be most unusual if they ever won a race, but I honestly believe that those are the type of boat racers who have more fun in the sport than the other competitors."

The Greatest Fans

No doubt, the least appreciated people associated with the sport of powerboat racing are families of the race boat drivers. They may not be directly associated with the racing, but they must share the financial burden and often travel with the race teams. One such person is Doris Johnson, wife of Skeeter Johnson.

"I miss it a lot," said Doris. "He was racing before I met him, and I liked it because we met so many people. It's like one big family. There were dances and dinners and parties. Of course it was all boat talk, but that was their lives. We traveled an awful lot. We took the kids everywhere, and saw some beautiful places. It could get hectic, and it could also get expensive, with the hotels and all. The sport itself was just an expensive hobby. I know it was a hard adjustment for him [Skeeter] to quit." During the annual regatta weekend today, the Johnsons still host other retired racers who visit as spectators.

Holly Baker, wife of driver Wheeler Baker, was once quoted as saying: "You can't have any reservations about your husband racing. I would be lying if I said I didn't worry somewhat, but I trust Wheeler's judgment and know he will not push the situation if it will endanger him or any other driver." Mrs. Baker has been involved with the sport of powerboat racing since she was seven years old. Now she sees her own children being raised in the powerboat racing world that has been a part of most of her life. "When the kids were little, I stayed home. As a mother I didn't want to drag the kids around with me," she said. "Now they are

Cambridge fans line the shore of Great Marsh for the annual Cambridge Classic powerboat regatta.

members of the little world of hydroplane racers which is comprised of very nice people who live together during summer weekends and become family."

Another wife of a veteran racer, Dorothy Oliver, was quoted in the *Evening Sun*: "It's all family oriented. The men do it, and the children grow up doing it. It's just the way boat racing goes." The wife of former national high point champion Chris Oliver added, "I don't really think racing is dangerous, although there are great speeds. Chris is a cautious driver. And all the drivers tend to look out for one another."

And the avid powerboat racing fans are a unique group. They follow the boat-racing circuit the same as any sports fan, but because of the lack of media coverage, they must often travel to the race site to keep up to date on how their favorite racers and boats are faring.

Billy Marshall, Curtis Warfield, Roy and Bobby Ruark, and Melvin Condon journey to Hampton, Virginia, and Valleyfield, Canada, each year to catch their favorite sport. In my opinion, Warfield probably has more knowledge of the sport of powerboat racing than anyone I have ever met. There are times when we, as boat-racing fans, like to test each other's knowledge and we play a trivia game. It is a very simple contest; we either give the name of a driver or the name of a boat and someone has to make a correct match. No one has ever beaten Curtis Warfield at this test of boat-racing trivia. I've thrown some obscure boat names at him, but he immediately responds with the correct driver.

Patti McMullen of Annapolis, APBA Region Four chief scorer, starts early in the morning of a sanctioned race preparing the "tons" of paperwork required for modern regattas. Nancy McMullen, APBA Region Four chief timer, is in the background awaiting the registration rush. Photograph by Joey Gardner

Another Dorchester County resident who has been considered boat racing's super fan for many years is Edgar Lewis. "I don't know of anything I like better than boat racing," he says. I like boats, slow and fast." His love for the water began early in his childhood while growing up in Dorchester County. He is from a five-generation family, which derived its livelihood from working on the water. Over the years, Lewis and his wife Jean traveled to Tonowanda, New York; St. Petersburg, Florida; Detroit, Michigan; and Dayton, Ohio; in addition to the Chesapeake Bay area regattas.

"I don't have any favorite boats or drivers, but I do bet quarters with the other retired racers," Lewis said. "I have no desire to race a boat because of my back trouble. I have a yellow streak that runs all the way up and down it," he chuckles.

Volunteers and Sponsors

Volunteers and financial sponsors of regattas are crucial. In the case of the Cambridge regatta, an auxiliary group, the Rudders, was formed in late 1981 to handle many of the logistical matters of race weekend, including concessions, programs, T-shirts, hats, tow money, and other administrative responsibilities.

The corn roast, which welcomes the racers and their families on Friday night, is coordinated by the Rudders. The first president of the Rudders, Charlene Burton, explained, "Friday night is the corn roast for the boat racers, pit crews and class sponsors. Saturday night we have a crab feast, and Sunday we have a barbecue for the participants." The sweet corn is donated by local farmers and cooked for the Friday night welcoming party. The crabs are donated by local watermen.

The Rudders give tow money to the racers to help take care of some of the expenses, such as motel rooms and gas. "Racers were given $3,000 in tow money if they had a legal start," said another former Rudder, Dodie Bromwell of the race in 1988. Each

Stu Shane of Havre de Grace watches as his 145-cubic-inch hydroplane HiJacker *is lifted off the trailer to be put into the Choptank River. The area of the cranes is referred to as "hot pits" and with the regulations of official racing only authorized persons are allowed in such areas. Photograph by Joey Gardner*

participant received an equal share of the total money we raised. This money came from the concessions sales and T-shirt sales," she added.

The remaining balance of regatta expenses at Cambridge are dependent upon local businesses. Some businesses become class sponsors. For a specific amount of money, they are given preferred acknowledgment in the annual program and are recognized over local radio station WCEM during the regatta. The largest overall contributor to the Cambridge regatta since 1982 has been J. C. Dodd Distributing Co., Inc. of Easton, a beer distributor. The arrangement between Dodd and the regatta was the result of a cooperative effort between then–regional sales manager Mike Reynolds of Anheuser-Busch, Jack Dodd, and CPBRA Commodore Robert Bromwell. Since 1982 the Cambridge regatta has been officially known as the Budweiser Cambridge Classic.

"But we could not operate without our local sponsors as well," says former CPBRA treasurer Allen Nelson. "Our class sponsors are extremely important to our being able to break even every year. Local businesses such as the National Bank of Cambridge have been strong supporters over the years."

Prize money is generally the largest expenditure of a regatta and in the case of Cambridge is about 25 percent of the total cost. Contributions, insurance, and supplies are also large expense items followed by survey fees, sanction and license fees, crane rentals, trophies, advertising, and food supplies.

In terms of income, the Cambridge regatta is quite unique. It does not charge admission for its spectators or charge for parking. These are usually the two largest areas of income for most regattas. Nelson explained, "We like the idea that we are providing our community with free family entertainment. The fact that it is professional sports entertainment is a bonus. This is an area of discussion we have every year and it would certainly help us financially to charge for admission and parking, but we are deeply committed to our tradition of a free event and as long as we are able to do so, we will continue with that tradition."

5

Risks and Dangers of the Thrill

The late racing great Bill Muncey was once asked to write a story about how he drives a hydroplane. He said, "It is an awesome sight and sound they (hydroplanes) present when they hurtle to the starting line, side by side, at exhilarating speeds down the front straightaway and into the first turn. As to personal preparation, I feel that if a man is going to play a game well, he had better play it very often indeed; he must virtually live it. It should go without saying that one must be in excellent physical condition and mentally alert. When asked, 'How do I drive a hydroplane?' I would answer, 'Very carefully.' "

Shortly thereafter, in 1981, Bill Muncey was killed driving a hydroplane very carefully. Since 1946, ten unlimited hydroplane drivers have been killed racing. In 1993 tragedy struck the Cambridge racing fraternity for the first time in eighty-two years of racing when Eddie Cannon was killed driving his 5-liter hydroplane *Wild Goose* in Hampton, Virginia.

Unquestionably, powerboat racing is a dangerous sport. The competitors are risk-takers in every sense of the word. Anyone who has seen a powerboat race, in person or on television, has witnessed some frightening accidents. Boats roaring across the water in excess of 100 miles per hour may suffer an explosive rollover or go airborne, seeming to do acrobatics in flight before plunging violently back into the water. It is a scary sight and usually has tragic consequences.

John Cobb was killed in 1952 while traveling at a speed of 206 miles per hour. And then there was "Black Sunday" on the Potomac River in Washington, D.C., in 1966. Ron Musson, a driver well known in the Chesapeake Bay region, was competing in the annual President's Cup Regatta in a boat named *Miss*

Ted Baker of Queenstown is about to go airborne in Skip Gillam's 280-cubic-inch hydroplane Last Blast. *Photograph by Tom Kelly.*

Bardahl when the boat suddenly disintegrated. Musson was killed instantly. Officials postponed the regatta for almost three hours before deciding to resume racing. Tragedy struck again in the final heat of the day when Rex Manchester in the *Notre Dame* and Don Wilson in the *Miss Budweiser* collided and both drivers died.

Serious accidents in powerboat racing cause enormous stress and anguish, not only to the injured driver and his or her family, but to regatta officials as well. Piles of paperwork must be completed for APBA national headquarters and insurance companies. Serious questions must be answered as to the cause of the accident. Was it driver error? Is the course too dangerous? What can we do to prevent this type of accident?

And it is all compounded when more than one person is involved. Skeeter Johnson handled his own mishap and injuries in 1968 at St. Petersburg, Florida, far better than he did a tragic accident some three years earlier. At St. Petersburg the accident involved only himself and fortunately his wounds would heal. But in June of 1965, Skeeter was in Virginia warming up for a 266-cubic-inch hydro race in the boat *Wa Wa*. He was flying at approximately 100 miles per hour down the front stretch when suddenly a boat inadvertently pulled out of the pit area into his path. Powerboats do not have brakes and even though Johnson did everything he could to avoid a collision, the *Wa Wa* plowed into the other boat. Driver Homer Bland was killed instantly, and Skeeter Johnson still lives with the pain.

All drivers know of the danger in the sport, and they become very irritated when asked if they have something like a death wish. One driver replied to such a notion, "Nothing is sillier than the notion that race drivers have a death wish. If you think so, you ought to look around at the people in motor sports. Most of them are enjoying life infinitely more than the average person."

Racers well known to Chesapeake Bay boatracing fans who have lost their lives in the sport include Homer Bland, Eddie Cannon,

Region Four has one of the most advanced rescue operation teams in the country, which includes fourteen certified divers as well as the volunteer emergency medical technicians. Note the Stoke's basket on the rescue boat that is used to safely lift an injured driver out of the water. Photograph by Joey Gardner

Dean Chenoweth, Lew Coehler, Frank Connally, Paul Flohn, Bill Heath, Mac Jordan, Frank Kossow, Hank Lauterbach, Tillman Mohr, Bill Muncey, Ron Musson, Jack McMahon, Bob Presley, Dave Sooy, and Dickie Webb. And yet legendary drivers such as Skeeter Johnson, who still has a metal plate in his hip from his racing accident, says he would like nothing better than to be able to get back into the cockpit of a raceboat and go racing.

The question "Why?" is always asked and the answer is always, "Because I enjoy it."

Two constant factors in motor sports persist: the quest for more speed and the search for the most rigorous safety environment. They are two contradicting goals.

Safety is certainly an important factor in powerboat racing. An individual interested in becoming a licensed APBA driver must first take a NASA physical examination. After receiving a physician's okay from a physical standpoint, the individual must then pass a driver's test. He must know and understand the rules of racing and be knowledgeable of the racing flags. He then must run practice laps by himself on the racecourse under the watchful eye of an official APBA referee. He may then be allowed to run in his first heat of racing, but he must run in last place and stay away from the other competing boats. This procedure will continue until the referee signs his competition card and recognizes him as a licensed driver.

In 1994 APBA made the most stringent rules change in recent years, requiring a reinforced cockpit for all classes of racing boats. The decision in favor of a reinforced and enclosed cockpit in racing has been controversial. One reason is the cost that the owners will have to bear to compete, and the other is the question of the effectiveness, particularly with regard to the enclosed cockpit. The

Bobby Brown of Parsonsburg in his stock 2.5-liter hydroplane Catch 22 *(S-22) with reinforced cockpit.*

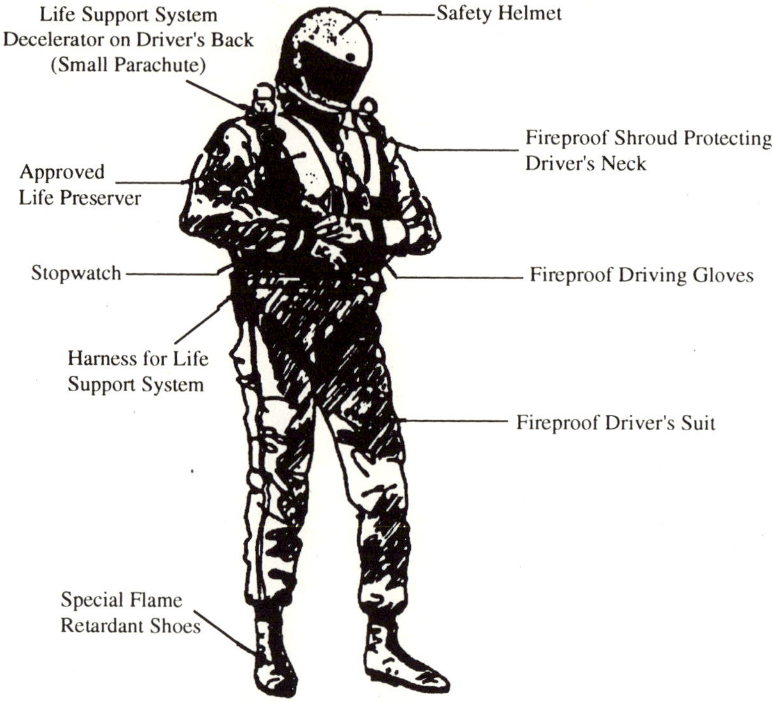

Required safety equipment for drivers

reinforced and enclosed cockpit technology was tested by APBA prior to implementing the rules changes. In both a roll-over and a flip accident, the driver was unhurt.

The first boats to use the new cockpits were the unlimiteds. Steve Reynolds did a violent barrel-roll in a race, but survived the incident, thanks to the enclosed cockpit in which he was strapped. The result of this new technology is in direct contrast to what drivers wanted to happen in the event of an accident in the early days of racing. In those days, they hoped they would be thrown

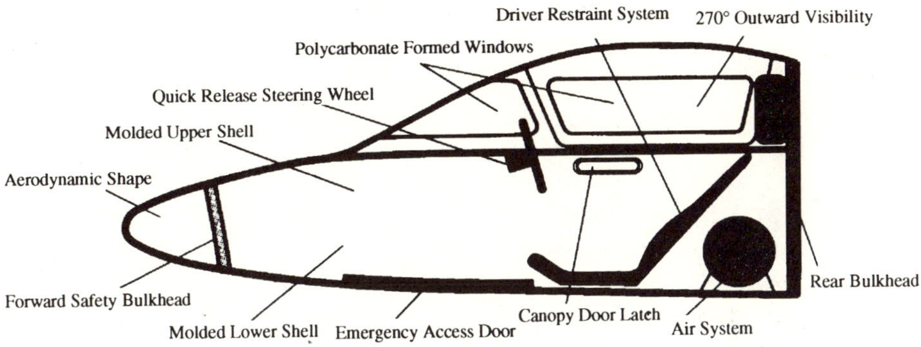

The enclosed driver capsule. Illustration courtesy of Ron Jones Marine

free of the boat. Of course they were not traveling over 150 miles per hour!

But a problem did arise from the reinforced and enclosed cockpit during a race in which Jim Kropfeld flipped over backwards. He was not injured, but nevertheless had mixed feelings about the experience of finding himself upside down in water, strapped to a seat and in total darkness. He reportedly could not find the escape latch to open the canopy. Rescuers extracted him by opening another escape hatch at the bottom of the cockpit.

Competitors using a reinforced cockpit also use a five-strap restraining system, and the boats must have enough buoyancy so that the combined hull, engine, and driver will still float in a swamped state. In addition, those boats with full-coverage canopies must have air-flow ventilation, adequate flotation for the cockpit section, a five-strap restraining system, and both internal and external release capability. Internal release capability isn't much good if the driver can't see to find the latch. So further studies will be done to refine the new equipment so drivers are not harmed by equipment intended to save their lives.

The safety factor has also directly affected the race committees today, as well as the drivers and the hulls. Not only is the safety of the competitors a compelling issue, but also the insurance costs and, in fact, the reluctance of insurance companies to participate in powerboat-racing events.

Many years ago, if an accident occurred on the racecourse, such as a boat turning over or a driver being thrown from a boat, the Coast Guard would be responsible for handling the incident. One retired driver recalls, "If you had an accident the Coast Guard would pull up to you and ask you your name. If you knew your name you would usually go back racing. If you did not respond or did not know your name they would pull you onto their boat—sometimes using a grappling hook. So what you didn't break in the accident was broken in the rescue operation."

That has all changed. All APBA-sanctioned regattas today require certified emergency medical technicians, certified divers, at least one ambulance, and at least one physician on site. If an accident occurs, a flare is fired, and racing stops. The rescue boat is a catamaran-type craft with a special all-aluminum davit that lifts the injured driver from the water to the boat in a Stoke's basket. An on-board crew of three medical technicians then administers emergency care with equipment such as an oxygen-powered resuscitator, a suction unit, and a bandaging machine. The driver is attended to by the EMTs and then returned to the pit area where he is seen by a physician. All of the safety operations are monitored by radio.

The Cambridge regatta committee is fortunate to have a former racer as their attending physician each year. Dr. Jimmy McCarter competed in the Pacific One Design class in 1948 with his own *Flyin Jimmy*. Each year, he now volunteers as the official APBA physician for the regatta, and, in addition to being available in case of an accident on the racecourse, he also treats many persons in the pit area and among the spectators for various complaints, such as bee stings and burns.

In 1983 John Fitzgerald of Rio Grande, New Jersey, got to know Dr. McCarter personally after taking a nasty spill in his

7-liter hydroplane *Leprechaun*. Fitzgerald later said, "Dr. Jim is Number One in my book, and the folks over at Dorchester General Hospital were super also. I hope I never have another accident like that, but if it happens, I hope it's in Cambridge." Fitzgerald retired from racing that year.

Chester resident Wheeler Baker has also had his brushes with catastrophe in the sport. In February of 1980, he was racing around a turn on the Lake Maggiore course when his hydroplane lifted off the water and flipped backward, throwing him aside. "It hung me in the air forever," he said. "I thought I was dead. I've always felt that a person needs a little brush with death to appreciate life," added the former Queen Anne's County Commissioner. "Anybody who races hard is going to go over once or twice. When a boat starts getting airborne on you, it just gets all quiet and still. You lose contact with the water. There's nobody but you and God, and you hope God brings you down."

Shown taking a turn in the Jersey Speed Skiff Selfish Pleasure *is driver Bill Salveson of Clermont, New Jersey, with riding mechanic Tom Herchenrider of King of Prussia, Pennsylvania. Photograph by Tom Kelly*

This sequence of photographs is clear evidence of the risk and danger in powerboat racing. Driver Andy Kachmarik flipped his super stock at a 1971 race in Atlantic Highlands, New Jersey. He was uninjured in the mishap, demonstrating the effectiveness of the safety equipment used by the racers.

6

Powerboat Racing's Impact on the Boating Industry

According to the National Marine Manufacturers Association, U.S. citizens spent $11.3 billion on boating in 1993. According to the Maryland Department of Natural Resources, Licensing and Consumer Services, there were 190,436 registered powerboats in the state of Maryland in that year. A 1995 study conducted by the University of Maryland showed that the boating industry creates over 18,000 full-time jobs, translating into $574 million in annual wages and income, which in turn generates $4.3 million in state and local tax revenue. An amount in excess of a billion dollars is spent in the state recreational boating industry. The same study, unveiled in Annapolis at the 17th Annual Maryland Trades Conference, estimates that about 15 percent of the state's tourism business came from boating and fishing. Most marine mail-order catalogs contain more than 10,000 marine items for sale.

All of which has a lot to do with the sport of powerboat racing, which has had a direct economic impact on pleasure boating, an impact that obviously affects a lot of people and their businesses.

Powerboat racing has for decades set the standard for every facet of the pleasure boating industry, from safety devices to bronze shafts to padding on the dashboard to trim tabs. In fact, powerboat racing is actually a testing ground for new innovations in the boating industry, most of which find their way onto the family runabout.

Probably the first development for the pleasure boating industry that was a direct result of racing affected the propeller. The first props were made of iron, but in racing a nonrusting bronze alloy was used. It didn't take long for the pleasure boating

Pat Cosgrove of Essex in his 7-liter hydroplane Last Fling.
Photograph by Tom Kelly

industry to pick it up. Not long afterward, the bronze shaft, a bar that transmits motion to the propeller, came to be used as well. The adoption in pleasure boats of struts to hold shaft and propeller more efficiently and cause less drag also came from racing.

Even the compass saw innovation and change by way of racing. Compasses were used primarily in endurance and offshore racing, and for years they would not stand much shock. They consisted of a floating unit in a fluid, such as alcohol and distilled water, until a racer decided to try Silicon and found the compass held up much better in rough waters.

Engine mounts were too easily broken in racing, so new mounts were designed especially for race boats. They also soon found their way into pleasure boat construction. Steering mechanisms were greatly improved as a result of racing. Trim tabs, which adjust the hull's floating position, appeared first on raceboats. The hand throttle was designed and developed in boat racing.

A number of the more familiar innovations in the pleasure boating industry came from boat racing. For instance, the APBA required that flotation devices be worn during competition long before the pleasure boat industry came out with styrofoam life jackets. Most of the ideas in seat padding came from boat racing—not so much for comfort as for survival. The contour seat was also designed for driver safety. Padded windshields and padded instrument panels were a necessity in boat racing and became a luxury for pleasure boaters. Boat racers started using trailers to haul their raceboats from regatta to regatta in the 1920s leading to their use by recreational boaters.

And, according to the old-time boat racers I talked to, perhaps the two most dramatic boat-racing innovations that impacted the pleasure boating industry were the shallow V-hull design and the use of fiberglass, although both claims are still matters of controversy. Some claim the V-bottom boat was developed in racing.

Others claim it is a holdover from the original skipjack with its straight frame throughout, which is why it is also referred to as a straight-framed boat and deadrise boat. But as far as racing is concerned, it clearly revolutionized the sport in terms of speed. With a V-bottom hull a boat could cut through the water much faster than if it had a flat bottom.

No one is quite sure whether fiberglass first impacted pleasure boats or raceboats. For that matter, no one even knows who built the first fiberglass boat. Tom Phillips of Owens-Corning says, "I know our guys in the lab built a fiberglass boat in the 1940s, but that was well before the boating or automotive industry started any production. The use of fiberglass in boating, and I mean boating in general, got going pretty well in the early fifties, and quite a few people claim credit for being the first. I think a company named Glaspar was one of the early fiberglass pleasure boat pioneers and in racing, the Bertrum story is fairly well known. But, who impacted who, I don't think is very clear-cut. I suspect they both really got going about the same time."

"The Bertrum story," Phillips refers to is the saga of Dick Bertrum of Miami, Florida, who supposedly went to Cuba in 1954 and had a raceboat built of fiberglass. As previously mentioned, however, I believe that Gordon Hoover raced the first fiberglass boat in 1959, and Bertrum started using the material for his boats in 1961.

As described earlier, DuPont introduced Kevlar in 1971 and it did not take very long for the boat-racing industry to try the new product. DuPont said, "Kevlar 49 aramid fiber is the most exciting boat-building material to come along since the development of fiberglass. It is the strongest synthetic fiber—five times as strong as steel, pound for pound! It is almost twice as stiff as fiberglass. The superior properties of Kevlar 49 allow boats to be built cost effectively, even with a 10x fiber cost. Typically, turnkey boat cost is only 10 to 15 percent higher, and that is more than offset by economy and longevity of operation."

Powerboat racing has also had an effect on the automotive industry. Better waterproofing of ignition systems was perfected more rapidly in powerboats than in automobiles. Powerboat racers also took to the V8 engines and the use of fiberglass before the automotive industry did. Today, as racing is adopting the latest technology in reinforced and enclosed cockpits, we may be seeing still another innovation for the pleasure boater.

Beyond the direct technological advances, boat racing has had an indirect, but positive, impact on the pleasure boating public. In 1983, twenty-six persons died in Maryland in boating accidents. Nine of those drowned simply for lack of a flotation device. Setting an example for those who engage in recreational boating, drivers and all officials at sanctioned regattas are required to wear life jackets on the racecourse. While alcohol figured in many of those 1983 fatal recreational boating accidents, alcohol is prohibited in the pit area of any APBA-sanctioned regatta. In an added effort to positively influence the boating public to the hazards of boating and the importance of safety measures, the Chesapeake Bay region's racers often attend boat shows, parades, and festivals to bring across those messages.

The late Harry Hargadon of Baltimore pilots his Jersey Speed Skiff Half Fast. *Photograph by Tom Kelly*

Cheri Petti is shown here in his 7-liter hydro Petti's Pet *leaving Cambridge Creek and heading for the Choptank River. The old Cambridge Shipyard is in the background.*

Three inboard hydroplanes racing on the Choptank River in Cambridge head into turn one on the old course in front of Long Wharf. The Emerson C. Harrington Bridge can be seen in the background.

7

The Future of Chesapeake Bay Powerboat Racing

Although powerboat racing has been around officially since 1903, the sport is struggling for survival. One school of racers is pushing for television sponsorship and big prize money, whereas another group wants to retain the "backyard" racing concept that has served so well for so long. An increasing number of "outlaw" clubs are popping up to stage their own races without a sanctioning body. Thus far, they are most popular in Florida and California. The number of regattas is dropping each year and the number of registered race boats is dwindling, due primarily to the high cost of the sport with no return on the investment.

One retired racer told me, "Today, it's more a question of matching dollars when it comes to racing. I imagine it was inevitable that powerboat racing would someday become commercialized. I don't mean that improvements in motors and hulls weren't to be expected—it isn't that at all. In fact, that not only benefits the sport of powerboat racing but benefits the boating industry as a whole which is vital to our Chesapeake Bay region. It's just that today a person can get caught up in a dollar race. In the thirties, forties, and fifties you could still find an individual who enjoyed racing a boat on his own merits."

These concerns will have their impact on all powerboat racing in the Chesapeake Bay region. In Cambridge, where the granddaddy of all Chesapeake regattas is based, the current race committee has a dilemma to deal with about which they must make a decision in the near future. The racecourse on Hambrooks Bay is threatened by the shifting and erosion of what was once Rooster Island. Winds and tides of many years have slowly "moved" the sand closer to the racing area, and each year the course must be altered for safety.

In 1989 Robert Bromwell commented, "Four or five years ago, we had over 300 feet between the course and Rooster Point. Now, the point has shifted so far onto the course, we have less than 70 feet. Due to the erosion of Rooster Island, and the shifting of Rooster Point onto the racecourse, the Cambridge Power Boat Regatta Association is in danger of losing its ability to get the race sanctioned by the American Power Boat Association."

As I completed this book, the local CPBRA was exploring several options for the future of the Cambridge Classic regatta. New sites were being evaluated and there was even talk of an "experimental" regatta to be held on Slaughter Creek at Taylors Island. There are once again rumors spreading that some type of breakwater, jetty, or structure may be constructed to help protect the rapidly eroding areas in Hambrooks Bay. The U.S. Army Corps of Engineers began a study on October 1, 1993, to help local officials deal with the Rooster Island situation with regard to its economic and environmental impact on surrounding land. Several project proposals were offered to local officials as a result of the study. Reportedly a letter of commitment to the corps will soon be written agreeing in principle to one of the proposed projects.

I have been a powerboat racing fan for almost fifty years and actively involved with APBA-sanctioned events in various capacities for twenty-eight of those years. I still love watching a race and still have the utmost respect for the competitors as true athletes. As with all sports, however, much has changed in boat racing. It's more difficult for the general public to get close to the drivers and boats today due to insurance regulations surrounding the pit area, and this can diminish interest. It will probably cost a potential driver about $30,000 to get into the sport today in most classes. And, yes, the media basically ignores the sport for some unknown reason. All of these factors militate against the future of boat racing in the region.

But I still look forward to going to Cambridge or Kent Island or Essex and picking my favorite spot to watch the race. Then I particularly enjoy waiting for the one-minute gun to sound to hear the thunderous noise as five to ten hydroplanes crank up their engines. Then comes my favorite time of a race—the start—when you look out over a body of water, such as the Choptank River, Back River, or Hog Bay, and see all those beautiful roostertails and hear the boats roaring together for a perfect start. I still don't have the answer to the question of why those of us in Cambridge are so touched by the sport of powerboat racing, but I do know that once it grabs you, it never lets go.

APPENDIX:
The Participants over the Years

The following appendix is a list of some of the Chesapeake Bay area drivers and the names/class of the boats they are most remembered for driving. Some drivers are listed several times since they gained fame in several boats/classes. There are also a few blanks in the chart that represent unknown facts about those particular boats.

Name	City	State	Boat Name	Boat Class
Pam Adams	Virginia Beach	VA	*Double Eagle*	1200 cc
Ed Alexanderwicz	Baltimore	MD	*Wee Tommy Tucker*	266 cubic inch
Bruce Ambrose	Chester	MD	*Satisfaction*	850 cc
Butch Ambrose	Aberdeen	MD	*Satisfaction*	145 cubic inch
George Applegate	Tasley	VA	*Flashpoint*	Jersey Speed Skiff
Gideon Baker	Chester	MD	*T-Riffic*	1 liter Stock
Ted Baker	Chester	MD	*Bo's Back*	225 cubic inch
Ted Baker	Chester	MD	*Last Blast*	5 liter
Tom Baker	Chester	MD	*Orange Crush*	Grand Prix
Tom Baker	Chester	MD	*Summit*	Grand Prix
Tom Baker	Chester	MD	*Deepwater Special*	Grand Prix
Wheeler Baker	Chester	MD	*Nudder Bo*	280 cubic inch
Wheeler Baker	Chester	MD	*Baker's Dozen*	7 liter
Wheeler Baker	Chester	MD	*Big Bird*	5 liter
Wheeler Baker	Chester	MD	*Miss Aquamet*	2.5 liter Modified
Steve Barrett	Pasadena	MD	*Hot N Nasty*	1200 cc
W. Lou Barrett	Cambridge	MD	*Evelyn M.*	
W. Lou Barrett, Jr.	Cambridge	MD	*Ava Lou*	225 cubic inch
W. Lou Barrett, Jr.	Cambridge	MD	*Home Brew*	225 cubic inch
Jim Batchelor	Annapolis	MD	*Gusto*	2.5 liter Modified
Jim Batchelor	Annapolis	MD	*Every Penny*	2.5 liter Modified
Bob Baxter	Baltimore	MD	*Gail*	145 cubic inch
Bill Block	North East	MD	*Block Buster*	48 cubic inch
Steve Bollman	Chester	MD	*Yellow Side Up*	Super Stock
Dick Briggs	Pasadena	MD	*Scarlett Thunder*	1 liter Stock
Dick Briggs	Pasadena	MD	*Sundancer*	Jersey Speed Skiff
Doug Brogden	Norfolk	VA	*Wanton Duchess*	145 cubic inch
Ralph Brogden	Hampton	VA	*Lil Injun*	Pacific One Design
Rodney Brodgen	Newport News	VA	*Kitty B*	225 cubic inch
Rodney Brogden	Newport News	VA	*Kitty B*	C Runabout
Raye Brohawn	Cambridge	MD	*Gypsy Girl*	Jersey Speed Skiff
Robert Bromwell	Cambridge	MD	*Flip Flop*	Jersey Speed Skiff
Robert Bromwell	Cambridge	MD	*Together Again*	Jersey Speed Skiff
Dave Bromwell, Jr.	Cambridge	MD	*My Girl*	2.5 liter Stock

Name	City	State	Boat Name	Boat Class
Bob Brown	Salisbury	MD	*White Lightning*	145 cubic inch
Bobby Brown	Parsonsburg	MD	*Lil Lightning*	2.5 liter Stock
Bobby Brown	Parsonsburg	MD	*Cloud Nine*	5 liter
Bobby Brown	Parnsonsburg	MD	*Catch 22*	2.5 liter Stock
Terry Browning	Virginia Beach	VA	*Paganga*	850 cc
Terry Browning	Virginia Beach	VA	*Miss Prime Mover*	7 liter
Bill Bunn	Baltimore	MD	*Renegade*	145 cubic inch
Greg Burton	Cambridge	MD	*Gypsy Girl*	Jersey Speed Skiff
Tom Butz	Germantown	MD	*Creme de Menthe*	Super Stock
John Callis	Virginia Beach	VA	*Stubborn Critter*	48 cubic inch
Eddie Cannon	Cambridge	MD	*Wild Goose*	5 liter
Jim Carr	Hyattsville	MD	*GoldieLox*	280 cubic inch
Bob Carrico	Laurel	MD	*Janine-Bean*	280 cubic inch
Walt Carter	Portsmouth	VA	*Gemini*	2.5 liter Modified
Bob Casey, Jr.	Stevensville	MD	*Night Crawler*	Jersey Speed Skiff
Joe Cheezum	Chester	MD	*Miss Zandy*	1.5 liter
Jim Coan	Springfield	VA	*Rubber Ducky*	280 cubic inch
Kim Corbman	Cambridge	MD	*Together Again*	Jersey Speed Skiff
Pat Cosgrove	Essex	MD	*Last Fling*	7 liter
Don Craig	Salisbury	MD	*Salisbury Stake*	1200 cc
George Cusick	Cambridge	MD	*Carol Ann*	136 cubic inch
George Cusick	Cambridge	MD	*Red Top*	145 cubic inch
Tom D'Eath	Cambridge	MD	*Southern Style*	150 cubic inch
Tom D'Eath	Fair Haven	MI	*Miss Budweiser*	Unlimited
Joe Danison	Havre de Grace	MD	*Nomad*	145 cubic inch
Frank Danser	Dover	DE	*Rowdy*	Pacific One Design
Jim Davidson	Havre de Grace	MD	*Unknown*	2.5 liter Modified
Jim Davis	Newport News	VA	*Gamma Ray*	150 cubic inch
Harry Dawson	Cambridge	MD	*Baby Lynn*	E Racing Runabout
Harry Dawson	Cambridge	MD	*The Thing*	C Racing Runabout
Don DeVault	Glen Burnie	MD	*Blue Blazes*	136 cubic inch
George Diering	Laurel	MD	*Chesapeake Lady*	7 liter
Jerry Donley	Annapolis	MD	*Pandamonium*	Ski Racing Runabout
Tom Donley	Annapolis	MD	*UFO*	Jersey Speed Skiff
Tom Donley	Annapolis	MD	*Punk*	Jersey Speed Skiff
Charlie Dunn	Washington	DC	*Miss Washington DC*	266 cubic inch
Don Dunnington	Silver Spring	MD	*Maryland Miss*	7 liter
Curtis Estes	Norfolk	VA	*Wa Wa Too*	280 cubic inch
Frank Foulke	Essex	MD	*Sagana*	225 cubic inch
Dennis Fowler	Baltimore	MD	*Rookie*	72 cubic inch
Jim Fyle	Baltimore	MD	*International IV*	266 cubic inch
Ken Germanhausen	Pasadena	MD	*Red Baron*	Jersey Speed Skiff
William Glazier	Cambridge	MD		D Racing Runabout
Lee Gore	Cambridge	MD	*Iron Eagle*	2.5 liter Stock
Lee Gore	Cambridge	MD	*Painter's Toy*	1.5 liter
Robert Green	North East	MD		B Service Runabout
James Haggett	Cambridge	MD	*Slipper*	

Name	City	State	Boat Name	Boat Class
Earle Hall	Hampton	VA	*Bluewater Special*	2.5 liter Modified
Harry Hargadon	Baltimore	MD	*Ruff Rider*	Jersey Speed Skiff
Ron Hearn	Hampton	VA	*Kitty B*	225 cubic inch
Ron Hearn	Hampton	VA	*Rudy's Comet*	150 cubic inch
Tom Horne	Hyattsville	MD	*Miss Agnes*	280 cubic inch
Steve Houmis	Norfolk	VA	*Came To Play*	2.5 liter Modified
Bill Hubbard	Cambridge	MD	*Miss Cambridge*	
Dan Huber	Baltimore	MD	*Ruff Rider*	Jersey Speed Skiff
Jim Huffman	Virginia Beach	VA	*Vertigo*	5 liter
Bobby Isaac	Eldorado	MD	*Paper Cup*	850 cc
Greg Isaac	Eldorado	MD	*Southern Cross*	280 cubic inch
Greg Isaac	Eldorado	MD	*Blitzkrieg*	280 cubic inch
Tommy Isaac	Eldorado	MD	*Paper Cup*	850 cc
Hugh James	Germantown	MD	*Drambuie*	Ski Racing Runabout
Phil Johnson	Cambridge	MD	*Destiny*	5 liter
Sarge Johnson	Cambridge	MD	*Sarge's Barge*	145 cubic inch
Sarge Johnson	Cambridge	MD	*Sarge's Barge*	7 liter
Sidney Johnson	Cambridge	MD	*Beverly Ann*	280 cubic inch
Sidney Johnson	Cambridge	MD	*Country Boy*	280 cubic inch
Sidney Johnson	Cambridge	MD	*Beverly Ann*	Jersey Speed Skiff
Sidney Johnson	Cambridge	MD	*Lil Angel*	Pacific One Design
Skeeter Johnson	Cambridge	MD	*Beverly Ann*	136 cubic inch
Skeeter Johnson	Cambridge	MD	*Wa Wa Too*	266 cubic inch
Skeeter Johnson	Cambridge	MD	*Beverly Ann IV*	280 cubic inch
Skeeter Johnson	Cambridge	MD	*First State*	280 cubic inch
Skeeter Johnson	Cambridge	MD	*Miss Washington DC*	266 cubic inch
Grason Jones	Cambridge	MD	*Heartbreaker*	6 liter
Grason Jones	Cambridge	MD	*Peppermint Twist*	Jersey Speed Skiff
Mac Jordan	Gloucester Pt.	VA	*Miss Sapphire*	225 cubic inch
Jack Keegan	Laurel	MD	*The Other Woman*	Ski Racing Runabout
Cynthia Kelly	Glen Burnie	MD	*Last Chance*	1200 cc
Barbara Kennedy	Bear	DE	*Afternoon Delight*	Jersey Speed Skiff
George Kennedy	Bear	DE	*Afternoon Delight*	Jersey Speed Skiff
George Kennedy, Jr.	Bear	DE	*Shameless*	2.5 liter Stock
George Kennedy, Jr.	Bear	DE	*Shameless II*	5 liter
Patti Kennedy	Bear	DE	*Lil Miss Metton*	1 liter Stock
John Kirschner	Baltimore	MD	*Miss Supersonic*	266 cubic inch
Sonny Kohr	Newport News	VA	*Chug A Boom*	2.5 liter
Frank Korsic	Silver Spring	MD	*Diana K*	Pacific One Design
Dan Kurth	Cambridge	MD	*Honolulu Baby*	145 cubic inch
Henry Lauterbach	Portsmouth	VA	*Wa Wa II*	266 cubic inch
Hank Lauterbach	Richmond	VA	*Something Special*	2.5 liter Modified
Larry Lauterbach	Chester	MD	*Gemini*	2.5 liter Modified
Larry Lauterbach	Portsmouth	VA	*Winston Eagle*	Unlimited
Norman Lauterbach	Portsmouth	VA	*Deejay*	Unlimited
Andy Lemeshewsky	Arnold	MD	*Wildcat*	280 cubic inch
Don Lewis	Baltimore	MD	*Scorpio*	5 liter

Name	City	State	Boat Name	Boat Class
Watson Lewis	Baltimore	MD	*Scorpio*	5 liter
Bobby Lockard	Havre de Grace	MD	*Paper Cup*	850 cc
George Loeb	Norfolk	VA	*Betty Gal*	48 cubic inch
Richard Loeb	Virginia Beach	VA	*Moonlighter Too*	2.5 liter Modified
John Loller	Baltimore	MD	*Bounty Hunter*	1 liter Stock
Frank Mallay	Baltimore	MD	*Miss Lulu*	7 liter
Frank Mally	Essex	MD	*Aqua-Dea*	7 liter
Bob Marsh	Annapolis	MD	*Friskie Too*	266 cubic inch
W.C. Martens	Hampton	VA	*Marbel*	135 cubic inch
James Martin	Hampton	VA	*B&G Auto Special*	2.5 liter Modified
Curtis Martins	Hampton	VA	*Marbel*	266 cubic inch
Doug Masengale	Glen Dale	MD	*Little Red Rocket*	2.5 liter Modified
John Mason	Washington	DC	*Hurricane*	280 cubic inch
Terry McArdle	Arnold	MD	*Slap Shot*	1 liter Stock
Gee McClain	Cambridge	MD	*Funny Feeling*	Ski Racing Runabout
Gee McClain	Cambridge	MD	*April*	Super Stock
Earl McMullen	Elkton	MD	*Five & One*	44 cubic inch
Keith McMullen	Edgewater	MD	*Plumber's Friend*	5 liter
Keith McMullen	Annapolis	MD	*Miss Gunsmoke*	1 liter Stock
Ken McMullen	Annapolis	MD	*Hostile Takeover*	1 liter Stock
Andy Miller	Baltimore	MD	*Tempest*	280 cubic inch
Chuck Miller	Queen Anne	MD	*Whoopee*	2.5 liter Modified
Chuck Miller	Landover	MD	*Wahoo*	1200 cc
Charlie Miller, Sr.	Annapolis	MD	*Whoopee*	2.5 liter Stock
Charlie Miller, Sr.	Landover	MD	*Dixie Boy II*	150 cubic inch
Fulton Moore	Cambridge	MD	*Taboo*	48 cubic inch
Bob Morris	Annapolis	MD	*The Other Woman*	Ski Racing Runabout
Brud Morris	Cambridge	MD	*Skee-Bo*	136 cubic inch
Ed Nabb	Cambridge	MD	*Black Magic*	Pacific One Design
Allen Nelson	Cambridge	MD	*Satisfaction*	1 liter Stock
Oscar Nelson, Jr.	Cambridge	MD	*June Bug*	48 cubic inch
Oscar Nelson, Jr.	Cambridge	MD	*Woody Boy*	E Racing Runabout
Jeff Niemyer	Baltimore	MD	*Sweetie Sue*	280 cubic inch
Chris Oliver	Millersville	MD	*Every Penny*	225 cubic inch
Chris Oliver	Stevensville	MD	*Every Penny*	2.5 liter Modified
Arthur Olsen, Jr.	Silver Spring	MD	*Hurricane*	280 cubic inch
Earle W. Orem	Cambridge	MD	*Segar*	225 cubic inch
Earle W. Orem	Cambridge	MD	*SeaGull*	225 cubic inch
Earle W. Orem	Cambridge	MD	*Sea Flea*	POD
Earle W. Orem	Cambridge	MD	*Sea Turtle*	225 cubic inch
Linwood Palmer	Lewes	DE	*Ca-Lyn-Ja*	136 cubic inch
Roger Phelps	Hampton	VA	*Skipper*	Pacific One Design
Roger Phillips	Hampton	VA	*Skipper*	Pacific One Design
Alton Pierson	Queenstown	MD	*Lil Barb*	136 cubic inch
Alton Pierson	Queenstown	MD	*Bo Bo Too*	280 cubic inch
Jo Ann Pliescott	Cambridge	MD	*Family Affair*	72 cubic inch
Elwood Pliescott, Jr.	Cambridge	MD	*Woody Jr.'s Special*	150 cubic inch

Name	City	State	Boat Name	Boat Class
Elwood Pliescott, Sr.	Cambridge	MD	*My Boy Woody*	D Runabout
Elwood Pliescott, Sr.	Cambridge	MD	*Woody's Special*	225 cubic inch
Jack Robson	Port Penn	DE	*Cricket*	2.5 liter Modified
Buddy Roper	Hampton	VA	*Kitty B*	225 cubic inch
Jim Ruark	Salisbury	MD	*Sweet Eileen*	2.5 liter Stock
Tom Ruark	Cambridge	MD	*Purple Haze*	Jersey Speed Skiff
Steve Schloss	Hampton	VA	*Windwalker*	5 liter
Valerie Schloss	Hampton	VA	*Pink Panther*	1 liter Stock
Louis Schneider	North East	MD	*Bob A Lou*	48 cubic inch
Louis Schneider	North East	MD	*Bob A Lou*	150 cubic inch
Vincent Schwing	Baltimore	MD	*Betty V*	7 liter
Jim Sexton	Edgewood	MD	*The Creeper*	Ski Racing Runabout
Stu Shane	Havre de Grace	MD	*Hijacker*	145 cubic inch
Stu Shane	Havre de Grace	MD	*Hijacker*	2.5 liter Stock
Steve Sharp	Havre de Grace	MD	*Bonanza*	145 cubic inch
Bob Shukert	Severna Park	MD	*Meant To Be*	5 liter
Bob Smith	Towson	MD	*Miss Pinky*	266 cubic inch
James Smith	Cambridge	MD	*Napinee*	
Mike Smith	Baltimore	MD	*Yellow Side Up*	Super Stock
Dick Snyder	Bethesda	MD	*Miss Wilson Line*	280 cubic inch
Don Starliper	Dundalk	MD	*Wee Cherie Too*	150 cubic inch
Jan Stepanek	Pasadena	MD	*Bandit*	Ski Racing Runabout
Bob Street	Baltimore	MD	*Good Vibrations*	6 liter
Bob Street	Pasadena	MD	*Hypertension*	2.5 liter Modified
Bob Street	Pasadena	MD	*Beg, Borrow & Steal*	280 cubic inch
John Sult	Portsmouth	VA	*Risky Business*	Super Stock
Bill Teat	Cambridge	MD	*Instigator*	Ski Racing Runabout
Bill Teat	Cambridge	MD	*Instigator*	280 cubic inch
Aubrey Thacker	Washington	DC	*Jezebel VIII*	D Runabout
Calvin Thomas	Baltimore	MD	*Breezy II*	225 cubic inch
Calvert Thompson	Chester	MD	*Wildcat*	Pacific One Design
Doug Thompson	Joppatown	MD	*Lil Doug*	145 cubic inch
Ed Thompson	Dundalk	MD	*TM Special*	E Runabout
Ed Thompson	Dundalk	MD	*TM Special*	1200 cc
Lem Thompson	Chester	MD	*Sandy K*	145 cubic inch
Ron Thompson	Joppa	MD	*Hot to Trot*	5 liter
Tom Thompson	Cambridge	MD	*The Gambler*	Jersey Speed Skiff
Tom Thompson	Cambridge	MD	*Super Chief*	5 liter
Tom Thompson	Cambridge	MD	*Hot Chocolate Too*	2.5 liter Stock
Tommy Thompson	Cambridge	MD	*The Gambler*	Jersey Speed Skiff
Henry Tieman	Wyoming	DE	*Here's Me*	Pacific One Design
Ed Townsend	Cambridge	MD	*Jittery*	E Racing Runabout
Ed Townsend	Secretary	MD	*Woody Boy*	E Runabout
C. Merritt Twilley	Salisbury	MD	*Miss St. Paul*	G Inboard Runabout
Dorothy Twilley	Salisbury	MD	*Miss St. Paul*	G Inboard Runabout
Jeff Tyson	Arnold	MD	*Pointblank*	Super Stock
Frank Vernon	Washington	DC	*Fancy Free*	150 cubic inch

Name	City	State	Boat Name	Boat Class
Walt Vickers	Cambridge	MD	*Pluto*	48 cubic inch
Don Waldorf	Newport News	VA	*Rowdy*	280 cubic inch
Key Wallace	Cambridge	MD	*Honker*	D Racing Runabout
Jack Welts	Bel Air	MD	*Juggernaut*	280 cubic inch
Jay Wheatley	Cambridge	MD	*Mud Flat Missle II*	Jersey Speed Skiff
Alan Wicker	Chester	MD	*T-Riffic*	1 liter Stock
Greg Williams	White Marsh	MD	*Hot to Trot*	5 liter
Durwood Wilson	Hampton	VA	*Sweet Pea*	280 cubic inch
Elliott Wilson	Cambridge	MD	*June Bug*	48 cubic inch
Jim Wilson	Hagerstown	MD	*The Outlaw*	1 liter Stock
Larry Wilson	Cambridge	MD	*Hot Pursuit*	145 cubic inch
Larry Wilson	Cambridge	MD	*Locomotion*	850 cc
Willard Wilson	Wilmington	DE	*Lil Lectron*	145 cubic inch
Dale Winazak	Salisbury	MD	*Skiffophrenic*	Jersey Speed Skiff
Dale Winazak	Salisbury	MD	*After Five*	5 liter
Raymond Wingate	Cambridge	MD	*Painter's Toy*	1.5 liter
Jim Wood	Cambridge	MD	*Blitz*	
Polly Wright	Cambridge	MD	*Scoundrel*	90 cubic inch
Chris Yewell	Queenstown	MD	*Sunset Heat*	1 liter Stock
Dan Ziegfield	Cockeysville	MD	*Miss Kris*	Super Stock
Ray Zulke	Baltimore	MD	*Alley Cat*	280 cubic inch

Index